Circling the Table

Circling the Table

The Spirit and Practice of
Roundtable Worship

William Johnson Everett

RESOURCE *Publications* · Eugene, Oregon

CIRCLING THE TABLE
The Spirit and Practice of Roundtable Worship

Copyright © 2024 William Johnson Everett. All rights reserved. Except for brief quotations in critical publications or reviews, no part of this book may be reproduced in any manner without prior written permission from the publisher. Write: Permissions, Wipf and Stock Publishers, 199 W. 8th Ave., Suite 3, Eugene, OR 97401.

Resource Publications
An Imprint of Wipf and Stock Publishers
199 W. 8th Ave., Suite 3
Eugene, OR 97401

www.wipfandstock.com

PAPERBACK ISBN: 979-8-3852-2238-4
HARDCOVER ISBN: 979-8-3852-2239-1
EBOOK ISBN: 979-8-3852-2240-7

VERSION NUMBER 05/30/24

Scripture quotations are from the New Revised Standard Version Updated Edition. Copyright © 2021 National Council of the Churches of Christ in the United States of America. Used by permission. All rights reserved worldwide.

Contents

In Gratitude | vii
Introduction | ix

1 Foundation Stones of Christian Worship | 1
    A Symbolic Action   2
    The Power of Metaphors and Symbols   3
    The Purposes of Worship   4
    The Longing for God's Governance   9
    Rehearsing God's Governance   10
    The Covenantal Drama of Worship   11

2 Symbolizing Governance: The Struggle between Monarchies and Republics | 14

3 Covenant and Republic: Toward a Symbol of Governance | 23
    Publics, Republics, and the Ecclesia   24
    Formation for Public Life: Participation, Pluralism, Equality, and Persuasion   26
    Publics Need Covenants   30
        Covenant and Constitutionalism   34
        Covenant and Federalism   35
    The Language of Governance   37
    Governance: Steering by the Mind of Christ   40

CONTENTS

    Presidency and Governance   43
    Election   45

4 Governance in the Image of the Triune God | 48

5 Worship in the Covenanted Public of Christ's Spirit | 60

6 Our Practice of Roundtable Worship | 69
    We Gather at the Table   73
    We Respond to the Call   76
    We Invoke or Confirm God's Presence   78
    We Remember   81
    We Give Thanks   83
    We Eat and Drink   84
    The Conversation   85
        The Readings   87
        The Talking Piece   88
        The Steward   89
    Prayers: The Wider Conversation   91
    The Commitments   95
    The Blessing and Sending   95

7 The Place of Roundtable Worship in the Wider Church | 97
    Of Size and Space   97
    The Circle Spirit in Larger Gatherings   100
    Language and Symbolism   102
    Gathering as Formation   104
    Diversity at the Table   108
    The Wider Circles of Engagement   108
    The Challenge of Ecological Reconciliation   110
    Interfaith Worship in the Abrahamic Traditions   111
    The Way Forward   112

Appendix: A Roundtable Liturgy | 115
Bibliography | 119

In Gratitude

I HAVE BEEN ENGAGED in some form of roundtable worship with my wife Sylvia for over thirty years. It is impossible to name all those who have enriched my understanding and our practice of worship in such a circle gathering as I seek to convey its practices and theological grounds in this little book. They have emerged, as the writer of Hebrews says, within a crowd of witnesses, some of whom I want to name on behalf of so many others. Kenneth Smits, OFM Cap., first ignited my understanding of the deep theological and ethical dimensions of worship. Thomas Porter anchored the roundtable in the practices and perspectives of restorative justice and encouraged me in the construction of round tables to create the setting for this circle of worship. I have been deeply enriched by the counsel of John de Gruchy and Robert Steiner, as well as the community of Rondebosch United Church in Cape Town, who have sought to live into this kind of worship, grounded in the processes of reconciliation. Ernst Conradie, also in South Africa, urged and encouraged me to deepen my understanding of the ecological dimensions of worship. Gerd Decke, my conversation partner and German translator over six decades, has continually stretched my horizon of ecumenical awareness as I tried to put my thoughts to paper. I have also been inspired and encouraged over the years by Kenneth Sehested, a co-founder of Circle of Mercy church in Asheville, NC, for many discussions about the work of molding poetry and liturgy in the struggle for justice,

IN GRATITUDE

peace, and faithful integrity. And finally, over the last twenty years my friends at the Roundtable at First United Methodist Church in Waynesville, North Carolina, have supported this venture over countless hours. I remember especially our fellow founding members Mel Harbin and Ken Johnson, now passed on to the greater conversation, as well as all those friends who have helped arrange the setting, bring food and drink, compose prayers, and spoke and listened with each other over these many years. In all of this, my wife Sylvia has added visions to these words as she has taken our conversation beyond the word with her artistic creations. To these and so many more I am deeply grateful. May the circle be unbroken in the coming years.

Waynesville, North Carolina
2024

Introduction

FOR OVER TWENTY YEARS a small group has gathered regularly at a round table in our church in the southern Appalachian Mountains. We are there for acts of worship that rehearse the drama of God's work of reconciliation in ways that don't generally appear in our ordinary worship services. In the course of our gatherings we speak together in prayer, remembrance, and thanksgiving. We taste of some bread and juice. We hear some Scripture along with insightful poems and readings. We sing some simple songs. We pass around a feather or bowl—a "talking piece"—to guide our speaking and listening in a circle of conversation. We lift up our voices in prayer. Finally, we reaffirm our commitments to the work of reconciliation. These are small and even gentle actions, but they are rooted in convictions that arise from the core of our Scriptural and communal traditions even as they overflow their usual bounds of thought and practice. This roundtable form of worship has had ripple effects not only in our congregation but in other churches and gatherings.

In this little book I want to introduce you to the practices of roundtable worship that we have come to enact in this setting. I also want to spell out my own understanding of the particular theological and ethical perspectives that ground and guide these practices. These perspectives have arisen in my theological work over the past forty years. This work has been fed by numerous theologians whom many readers will see standing in the wings, voicing both their affirmations and their own questions. I will not seek to re-do or recite their work here. What I want to do here is assemble and to some extent rework my own theological understandings as they are expressed in this particular form of worship. The perspective at work here introduces concepts and views that may well be unfamiliar to many readers. Moreover, the way these perspectives come together in this pattern of roundtable worship may be quite jarring or even contradictory to some people's usual understandings and practices of Christian worship. Let me emphasize that these are my own understandings, which have arisen to guide my convening of this worship group. The participants who have shared in this experience have their own often overlapping views, which have helped shape mine, but this little book does not presume to speak for them. What it does seek to do is stimulate ongoing deep theological reflection on this core work of worship in the Christian tradition, a tradition open not only to other religious patterns but to the wider publics in which we live.

The understanding I will seek to lay out here emerges from my long-standing effort to reflect on the ethical meaning of worship.[1] I have not been interested merely in seeing how worship might motivate us to ethical action, but how our ethical perspectives and convictions actually emerge out of the deep symbols and rituals of our worship. Not only does worship form a foundation for our ethical outlook and action, but ethics can and ought to shape efforts to transform worship so it has more ethical integrity. The relation of ethics to worship is a reciprocal one.

Within this engagement between ethics and worship, I have lifted up the way models and values of governance lie at the heart of the grand tradition of both Jewish and Christian (and indeed, I think, Muslim) worship. Therefore, any effort to appraise or transform our worship should take seriously the long traditions of political theory that have shaped our history. This is a very significant claim that lies far from most people's understanding and

---

1. For earlier expressions of this effort see Everett, *God's Federal Republic*; Everett, *The Politics of Worship*; and Everett, "Gathering at the Roundtable," in Porter, ed., *Conflict and Communion*, 121–130.

experience of worship. For many people, especially in the broad Evangelical stream of American Christianity, worship is a practice for nourishing each individual's personal struggle toward salvation. It is a drama about their personal life of sin, repentance, forgiveness, and promise of new life. What I will describe in this little book is an approach to worship which interprets this personal struggle within our contemporary understandings of wider social, political, and even cosmic dimensions of our life.

People who seek to understand, interpret, and reform worship have long turned to psychology, anthropology, literary criticism, and history to inform their efforts. My engagement with political theory as well as law and jurisprudence in order to understand worship may strike some people as odd or even wrong-headed. Anything, they say, that smacks of politics, government, or law should have no mention in worship! I hope that these pages will be able to show how perspectives on governance have a profound significance for Christian (as well as Jewish) worship. They are rooted not only in the biblical origins of our worship but in the long history of the church, both for good and for ill. The struggle for God's justice cannot avoid the question of how we think about the widest reaches of the way we govern our lives. It is in worship that we try to sense what this structure of justice and governance might mean and begin to structure our lives around these visions.

This centrality of governance imagery in worship speaks specifically to some core ethical commitments of the participants in these gatherings. Long-time participants in this roundtable worship have been shaped by extensive involvement in efforts to overcome the many forms of injustice grounded in distinctions of biology, whether of sexual difference, gender roles, or race. In all of these efforts, we are struggling to articulate a social, ethical, and theological vision that integrates these biologically based distinctions into a wider fabric of citizenship in God's great creation, indeed, as I would say, in God's great republic. This means we have struggled to transform our worship from patterns permeated with images of male dominion, whether in families or kingdoms, to forms of democratic, republican, and constitutional order which evoke our allegiance in our daily lives as citizens.

Most people are familiar with these efforts to move from hierarchical orders of domination to circular patterns of democratic, conciliar self-governance. In our own time the roundtable has become a symbol of conversation and negotiation in the collapse of empires, tyrannies, and dictatorships. As early as the 1930s, E. Stanley Jones was convening roundtables to bridge divisions among India's religious groups, while Mahatma Gandhi was participating in roundtables to begin the process of liberating India from British imperial rule. When the Berlin Wall fell in 1989, taking the East German regime with it, people gathered at roundtables to debate their democratic future. Since then, roundtable discussions have pervaded not only the media but also local community-building efforts around the world.[2]

One of the key features of this great effort of political reconstruction has been the development of practices of restorative justice. Over against the retributive justice that has accompanied these systems of domination, people have embraced efforts to transform conflict and the violation of social norms through restorative practices of apology, forgiveness, re-inclusion, participation, and healing. It is these particular practices of restorative justice, especially those of the circle conversation, that lie at the heart of the worship practices I am lifting up here. They are the lens through which we seek to understand the justice and governance of God.

My own perspectives on theology, ethics, and worship have been shaped by an immersion in several streams of Christian tradition. I was raised in the Evangelical tradition of both traditional and progressive Baptist churches but was soon introduced to the rich liturgical traditions of the Episcopal church at the Washington National Cathedral and then led into the heart of Roman Catholic sacramentalism through my fifteen years of teaching at St. Francis Seminary in Milwaukee, Wisconsin. In mid-life I found a denominational home in United Methodism's expansive tent and been

---

2. I reviewed this development extensively in Everett, *Religion, Federalism, and the Struggle for Public Life.*

anchored there ever since. In addition, I worked as a consultant for many years with Lutheran church bodies in Germany and Geneva, Switzerland, imbibing the doctrinally rich worship traditions of those churches. Along the way I have been continually drawn to appreciate the spirituality of the meetings of the Society of Friends as well as other intentional religious communities. Sabbatical sojourns in India and South Africa have further enriched this stew of ecumenical worship experience. In addition, the spiritual traditions of the Cherokee and other indigenous peoples, with their images of the hoop and the circle at the heart of all life, have come to form yet another layer of awareness in the development of my vision of worship. Elements of all of these sources have contributed to my understanding of worship around our table and to the actual construction of round communion tables in my later years.[3]

The importance of this kind of worship and the model of restorative justice it embraces is only heightened by the contemporary assault on democratic, republican, and constitutional norms of governance. Whether by hereditary monarchs in the Middle East or tyrants, dictators, demagogues and despots of all stripes and nations, we are besieged by those who would destroy conciliar consensus-building, truth-seeking, and our nascent efforts toward restorative justice. These political forms of domination are echoed in efforts to bring back a very patriarchal form of family and interpersonal life. It may be we could enter a long winter of tyranny. Or we might be on the verge of a vivid recovery of governance that brings people together in genuine dialogue and a search for the common good. In either case, a worship that preserves our longing for this governance will continue to be a core spiritual experience of personal and corporate renewal.

For this exploration, I will begin with some foundational affirmations about the process, purpose, and key metaphors of governance shaping Christian worship. They are presuppositions that emerge from long consideration by many others as well as myself, but I do not undertake to lay them out in detail here. My

---

3. I have reviewed this development in Everett, *Making My Way*. My tables can be viewed at http://WisdomsTable.net and http://WilliamEverett.com.

primary interest is to be clear about these foundational principles rather than to be scholarly in their exposition. I have included some footnotes for those who want to probe more deeply into various foundational discussions, but it is not my intent to argue them out fully here.

I then spell out what it means to talk about patterns of governance in relation to worship. In particular, I will summarize arguments I have made elsewhere about the struggle between models of patriarchal monarchy and the constitutional republican and democratic orders that enlist our loyalty today. This is a long conflict going back to Biblical accounts and running throughout Western history, gaining a bloody articulation in the wars of religion as well as the English Civil War of the seventeenth century. It is a struggle that continues to this day.

Drawing on earlier work, I will lay out more specifically the contours of this contemporary vision of governance as it is rooted in both biblical and Western history. At the heart of this vision is the concept and activity of "covenantal publicity," which draws together key elements of both the Bible's covenant tradition and concepts of public life reaching back to the ancient Greeks and Romans, gaining fresh articulation today through the work of Hannah Arendt, Jürgen Habermas, Daniel Elazar, and many others.[4] I will flesh out this central concept in Chapter 3.

Governance is not simply a secular concept about power and authority in our present world. It also is a concept that opens us up to the way God relates to us within the whole of creation. In speaking of "God's governance" we are pointing to the way God orders our world. The concept of governance directs our gaze toward the way we exist in relationships of power and authority in every dimension of our lives. At the same time, it can direct us back to the very character of this governing God. It does this by directing us to the way our understanding of governance is grounded in our deeper commitments. Governance, unless it is

---

4. The key works are Arendt, *The Human Condition*, and Arendt, *On Revolution*; Habermas, *The Theory of Communicative Action*; and Elazar, *The Covenant Tradition in Politics*.

reduced to the mere exercise of violent force, depends on persuasive arguments and deep symbols for its legitimacy. Without legitimation, without being able to show how its structures and policies are rooted in deep common convictions, government loses the authority that enables it to order human groups on a largely voluntary and self-regulating basis. Legitimacy is lost when judges are moved by personal reward rather than adherence to the underlying rules of legal reasoning. Priests who curry the favor of the wealthy weaken the legitimacy of a church that is founded on a preference for the poor and oppressed. The task of legitimation and re-legitimation is a constant challenge.

This work of legitimation inevitably drives us back to our foundational commitments and understandings about the nature of human life and natural order, indeed to the wisdom of the God of all creation. This is how governance has always been grounded in some kind of worship, whether in being directly "religious" in its character or indirectly, as in the "civil religion" that arises in many contemporary democracies. In the end, these arguments for legitimation of government push us to our understanding not only of nature but of "nature's God," as the founders of the American republic put it. And so in the next part I lift up the way Christian understandings of God have evolved in a trinitarian argument that moves from a hierarchical, pyramidal image of the "persons" of the Trinity to a circular dynamic rooted in the energy of love. This shift in our understanding of Trinity has profound importance for our understanding of just governance and political order.

Grounded in this trinitarian understanding I then spell out a vision of church that incorporates these elements of theological vision and covenantal publicity. This vision of the church provides the basic grounding in which our understanding of roundtable worship finds its life.

I will then lay out and reflect on the practices of our roundtable worship in light of the basic commitments and understandings of the earlier chapters. For those who would like to form and convene gatherings of roundtable worship, I have prepared a compilation of liturgical elements I have written over the past twenty years. *Words at Table: Liturgies for Roundtable Worship* is available in paperback and Kindle formats through Amazon.com. It contains numerous calls, invocations, thanksgivings, and prayers for many themes and seasons in the church year. Under a Creative Commons license, they can be used easily in a variety of worship settings.

I conclude this volume with some reflections on the limits and further lines of possible development for this form of worship, including its pivotal role in the continual revitalization of the life of the churches and their environing societies.

Some readers may want to begin with the description of roundtable worship in chapter 6 and then return to chapter 1 to begin exploring the theological foundations of roundtable worship. In either case, I hope I can help you see the connections between the little public of the table and the great republic of God's governance throughout creation.

1

Foundation Stones of Christian Worship

CHRISTIANS WORSHIP IN A tradition that stretches back over three thousand years to the ritual practices and symbols of the ancient Hebrew people. My own reception of this tradition is shaped by the Bible as well as church practices that sought to recover this biblical tradition in the Reformations of the sixteenth century, and more recently, in Roman Catholic life. Above all, the perspective and practices I trace out in this little book have been formed by the grand narrative of biblical vision that focuses on the ultimate fulfilment of God's beloved creation. It is a vision strung out from Genesis to Revelation. It is a visionary drama that lies at the heart of our worship.

I begin with a set of foundational assumptions about Christian worship. Some involve the concept of worship in general. Others constitute the theological basis for my construction of this particular vision of roundtable worship. First, let me identify three foundation stones for the way I approach worship generally.

A Symbolic Action

Worship is a *symbolic action* that takes the ordinary realities of our life and uses them to help us engage the transcendent realities at work in our lives. In worship we try to envision and live into, in some dramatic way, the ultimate ground and goal of our lives, indeed of all creation. Because we are dealing with something that goes far beyond our intellectual or psychological capacities, we have to take the known objects, images, and events of our life—bread, water, love, sorrow, stones, colors, weddings, births, and deaths—to represent in some way the divine life beyond us.

We do this not only through objects like a cross or a candle, but also through actions like singing, walking, standing, kneeling, eating, gesturing, and dancing. We construct spaces, whether in caves, fields, buildings, or open stadiums, that shape the way we gather together and orient ourselves to some actions or objects that bind us together in a common vision or voice.

Symbols are not merely signs that point to the transcendent realities by which we live. They are also a means by which we are shaped by that reality. In this sense, they have a sacramental power that re-shapes our lives in accord with the mystery that lies beyond us. They have emotional as well as intellectual depth and power. They bring together our vision and our action, our concepts and our emotions. Worship is not simply a speech event that teaches our minds but an emotional, dramatic event that shapes our emotional loyalties, our longings, and our habits of action.

By saying that worship is an action, I want to lift up the way it is a kind of drama. It depends on scripts like prayers, sermons, scriptural readings, songs, and the like, but it is also a kind of choreography, a kind of dance, in which our bodies enact what these words point to. Each worship has a dramatic script, just as the church year seeks to spell out the grand drama of God's creative and saving work.

The Power of Metaphors and Symbols

As a symbolic activity worship relies on metaphors to guide our action and belief. Metaphors are projections of everyday reality onto the divine mystery. Arising from our ordinary common life, they become elaborate symbols in the extraordinary world of life-transcending ritual. The ritual action becomes a kind of heaven in which they gain emotional power and more universal significance. They gain deep meaning within the context of the larger vision of salvation.

It is crucial that we recognize how these symbols inevitably come back to earth to attach this heavenly power to the patterns of life in which we live. They return to earth with their heavenly power to legitimate our life in family, economics, government, warfare, and science by grounding them in ultimate cultural values. For instance, in this dynamic process of legitimation the father of whom Jesus spoke rises up to symbolize God and returns to earth with transcendent powers to establish the primacy of the father in ordinary family life. The "talent" in Jesus's parable becomes a symbol for our entire earthly vocation. The king of earthly realms rises into the heaven of religious symbols and comes down to earth to bless the men who take the thrones of earth's dominions. The mother of ordinary homes becomes the "Queen of heaven" who now seeks to be brought back down to earth as Wisdom, healer, and the everlasting arms of consolation. It is a cycle that has gone on throughout religious history.

In discussing worship—and this is crucial for my argument in this book—we have to take into account this cycle of metaphoric ascent and symbolic descent. We have to be aware of the way we use metaphors from the world around us to construct symbols for the divine and also the way those very symbols gain a heavenly charge to sacralize in some way the patterns of life that have arisen in human culture and history. Worship is not only a way we are led into transcendent mysteries but also the way our images of those mysteries shape and undergird our present life, not only as individuals, but even more broadly as institutions and whole societies.

Worship is not only the words to address God but the language of power and authority that shapes our everyday lives.

Some of these symbols—these charged and complex metaphors—gain a general power to shape not only our relation to God but also to many different sectors of our life. The symbol of "father," for instance, has gained a power from its association with the divine that extends not only to family life, but to politics (the "father" figure), to the country ("patriotism" derives from the Latin for father), to the figure of the paternalistic business owner, to the "Founding Fathers" of our Constitution, and many other areas of social life.

This is why we need to take responsibility for our worship as an ethical act. These symbols act not only as ways to imagine God and God's ultimate purposes but also as foundations for our ordinary life in family, government, economics, and social life. This is how religious worship helps legitimate our ordinary social, economic, and political institutions. We need to account for this worldly impact from an ethical standpoint. Worship is the act of imagining our ethical future. It works at the very foundation of our ethical vision as well as our daily life.

The Purposes of Worship

In thinking about worship and its ethical impact we inevitably come to the question of its purpose. What functions does it serve in human activity? What functions should our own worship as Christians seek to serve? How we answer these questions shapes a great deal of the way we approach the design and conduct of worship. As I have thought about this question over the years, I have identified four functions of worship. Worship patterns vary significantly, depending on which function is primary for the worshippers. These functions are *education, motivation, representation*, and *rehearsal*.

The first perspective sees worship functioning as *education*. This purpose is deeply embedded in churches originating in the Protestant Reformation. In a world of illiteracy, widespread superstitions, and an often magical understanding of worship, the sixteenth-century reformers in Germany, Switzerland, and the Netherlands focused worship on the exposition of Scripture. They developed catechisms to instruct the people and used the sermon as the central point of access into participation in the divine economy of salvation. All adornments, gestures, and rituals that might distract from a hearing and understanding of God's Word were stripped from worship. The sanctuary, as in Calvin's Geneva, became an auditorium. Among divines in England and America the sermon became a model of rigorous thinking, exposition, and explanation. Lying behind this enormous development of the sermon as the centerpiece of worship was the belief that right understanding was indispensable to a right response to God. An understanding conformed to God's Word could shape and guide the will to right action. The Word could and should rule the will. Or could it? An awareness of the limits of rational understanding led preachers in the Reformed tradition, like Jonathan Edwards, John Wesley, and George Whitefield, to craft sermons that would also move the heart. The test of a sermon's impact became its capacity to move the audience to repentance, conversion, and a new way of life. Worship became an act of motivation.

The purpose of worship as personal *motivation* is best represented in the Evangelical and Revivalist traditions of the eighteenth and nineteenth centuries, both in England and America. In particular, especially on the American frontier, worship was focused on radical conversion of individuals who could then form congregations. Churches in America became voluntary associations far removed from the parish jurisdictions of England. They had to revive and motivate people to form independent Christian communities. And, of course, this was the primary function of worship in the missionary churches of the non-European world. The chief purpose of worship became motivational. It was to affect emotion and the heart. Like the educational model, it was focused on preaching, but not the declarations of a clergy with a scholar's grasp of the Scriptures as much as the charismatically inspired exhortations of a preacher.

Motivational worship functioned to address individuals who were often disconnected from the old communities of kinship and ethnicity. It sought to strengthen individuals to survive in the rapid mobility of society in the industrial era. It formed people capable of participating in the expanding market economy of capital accumulation. Motivational worship, through spirited songs and passionate rhetoric, aimed at cultivating personal virtues that might guide people in this maelstrom of social change. At the same time, this motivational worship could also rescue those caught in systems of oppression, whether as impoverished immigrants in industrial cities or the enslaved Africans at the heart of America's Southern agriculture and, derivatively, of Northern commerce. But the heightened emphasis on individual experience can easily obscure the dominant biblical focus on God's work of seeking to order human affairs and the whole creation according to the divine purpose. For example, in the relation of Protestant churches (both Black and White) to the civil rights movement, there was little or no discussion either of the issue of gender inequality in church life or of the possible contradiction between the monarchical structure of power in many churches and their members' fervent hopes for a fuller democracy.

At the same time, the songs, prayers, rituals like baptism and communion, personal testimonies, and above all fervent preaching could energize, transform, convert, and empower the participants to work both individually and collectively to resist injustice and create justice in the world around them. The way African American churches empowered the civil rights movement in the 1960s represents this approach most dramatically. Personal, communal, and ecclesial interests all coincided in the drive for civil equality in American public life. The liberation of this relatively unified community could draw on powerful biblical themes of exodus, restoration, resurrection, and Pentecost. To the degree that worship becomes a kind of vivid re-enactment of these dramatic themes it leads us to the third perspective, that of worship as representation.

In this perspective worship is the *representation* of the divine order of things. God, the work of salvation, the life, death and resurrection of Christ, and the incoming of the Holy Spirit–all of these are re-presented in worship. Worship is the mirror of the divine life that orders and redeems creation. Such a view permeates much of Roman Catholic, Orthodox, and Anglican tradition, where the re-presentation of the sacrifice of Christ on the cross takes center stage in the drama of worship. Worship is so richly symbolic precisely because it seeks to make the richness of the divine life available to us. The focus is neither on the participating individuals nor on their task of worldly action but on God's action as re-presented in the worship itself. This usually implies that just as God is eternal and unchanging, so also must the liturgy be. God's holy transcendence is then interpreted more in terms of unbroken tradition than of opening us up to a transformed new creation.

The representational approach, though providing symbols that evoke hope in a transformed existence, often pays little attention to the actual transformation of persons or communities, let alone of non-religious institutions. The crucial point is merely that God's eternal pattern of right order is rehearsed in symbolic ways–ways that over time often become quite distant from the social patterns and symbols in which the church exists. Moreover, they can become quite distant from any prophetic or ethical critique generated by biblical preaching.

However, this is not inevitable in this approach. I am reminded here of what the Jesuit priest and paleontologist Pierre Teilhard de Chardin did with the traditional Catholic Mass. Out on the wind-swept sands of the Ordos desert of China, where he worked with others to transform our understanding of human origins, he had no bread or wine to celebrate the Mass. In any event the meaning of those two elements had often been reduced to a mechanical action by a priest removed from the people and their actual lives. So he took the earth around him and declared it the Body of Christ, which has been broken up for us. And he took the actual suffering of the earth and its peoples as the blood of Christ which transforms the world.[1] He thus vividly changed our understanding of our place in the universe and the way God's saving work was the energy of the whole evolutionary process. The traditional Mass, which had become a rote performance, received a deeply personal as well as ecological and cosmic meaning. This was a creative act of worship change in the representational mode.

All three of these perspectives have their strengths as well as their limits. The educational model forms analytical minds that can clear away the idolatries of unworthy devotions, but it can leave the heart cold and not strike sparks at the hearth of human motivations. It can establish the basis for a clear ethical and legal order but can easily lead to a merely judicial understanding of sin, grace, and salvation. The motivational model can certainly energize people for individual action but it tends to neglect the way patterns of worship themselves lift up models of future existence as well as reinforce people's existing patterns of action in families, work, or civil institutions. The representational model can freeze liturgical action into the rote replication of seemingly eternal paradigms rather than help us imagine God's opening up of new possibilities for our life.

A fourth functional perspective, that of *rehearsal*, draws on the strengths of these three but seeks to form people more intentionally to participate in the dramatically new order of God's justice, shalom, and reconciliation. Like the others it has theological warrant as well as cultural appropriateness. The line of argument pursued in this book sees worship as the rehearsal of God's right order. It recognizes the importance of affirming a divine purpose and ordering of creation but also the need for our participation in it. It recognizes the importance of learning the "scripts" provided by our biblical heritage but it knows that we have to enact them dramatically if they are to reshape our lives. Worship as rehearsal affirms the essentially public character of worship as an experience held in common. It is not merely an experience

---

1. The complete "Mass on the World" is in Teilhard de Chardin, *Hymn of the Universe*, 19–37.

contained in the individual or performed by the priestly leader but a drama in which all participate.

The metaphor of drama at work in this perspective also affirms the constructed character of our life as well as of our worship. This dramatic action schools people's capacity for improvisation, reworking, collaboration, and actual performance. Our virtues of patience, humility, honesty, forgiveness and the like are cultivated in the rehearsal of relationships and narratives presented by regular worship themes. Some of these are biblical stories of prodigal sons and forgiving fathers. Seasonal events like Lent can school us in self-examination, patience, and forgiveness. Christmas pageants can shape our roles as mothers, fathers, and ordinary workers open to miracles and wonder.

Crucial to the language of rehearsal is its recognition that all our worship is ultimately provisional. It awaits the final unfolding of God's purposes. The gap between heaven and earth is the gap between now and not yet. This is the gap in which ethics functions to shape actions grounded in the past but oriented toward a possible new future. Worship is essentially eschatological, it is an opening to the future, even as it celebrates the presence of the future through its symbolic action.

These, then, are four basic starting points for how I understand worship. It is a symbolic activity rooted in key metaphors that guide our rehearsal of the story of God's unfolding purpose for creation. What then, are the crucial symbols, metaphors, and patterns of rehearsal that underlie the kind of worship I am presenting in this book? I want to identify three additional stones that are the foundation for this perspective.

The Longing for God's Governance

Biblical faith is the search for God's right governance of our lives, indeed of all creation. It is a search for God's ultimate ordering pattern and power. It begins with the ordering of the primordial chaos by God's Spirit and then gains explicit form in God's giving of a "law"—a Torah, a teaching, a "Word" and a Wisdom to live by. It is given as covenant, that is, as a set of promises by God to a group of tribes struggling for unity and freedom. So this pattern is from the outset a work in progress, as we say today. It is always something that is our foundation as well as an anticipation of future realization. We confront then, not only a promising God but a political one, a God seeking to realize an order of right governance for our lives. The making, keeping, breaking, and renewal of this promise constitute the warp and weft, indeed the whole unfolding historical tapestry, of God's work of salvation. Our faith is a search to play our proper role in the drama of this covenantal history.

Rehearsing God's Governance

In this light, worship becomes the rehearsal of our life within God's overarching governance. It is the way we try on this drama and the roles it offers us as individuals, as groups, and as whole peoples. It is both a way to help us see the patterns of God's creative process in our life and also a way to anticipate the ultimate realization of the promises already embedded in our lives. It is a way to live into the scripts of this salvation drama, whether they offer us scripts of repentance, of humility, of service and self-giving, of gratitude, or courage in the face of adversity.

As a rehearsal of God's governance, worship also invites us into ritual actions and symbols that dramatize the relationships of power and authority that govern our lives. Whether it enacts relations of kings and subjects or constitutions and citizens, it lays out fundamental attitudes, aspirations, and patterns of action that reach out into our wider society to give legitimation to how we order our lives today. It can also serve to undermine accepted orders of governance by providing alternative patterns of assembly, of obedience, of authority, and change. The symbolic drama of the "cult" at the heart of worship thus becomes the patterns for our "culture," whether in prophetic critique or patient improvement.

It is important to note that this drama, along with the realization of its promise, is not simply about liberation from oppression in its many forms. It is not simply about the struggle to participate in the beloved community or the promised land. Following ancient Israel, it goes further. It tries to envision the structure of relationships in which power and authority is exercised for the common good. It involves a vision of how our relationships are constituted according to God's intention for the creation. In short, it involves our vision of governance, that is, of the way God seeks to order the universe, including our human relationships. Without this vision of a structure for our relationships, liberation simply falls back into whatever forms of domination originally shaped and captured us. We return to a Pharaonic Egypt rather than enter a new life in a promised land.

The Covenantal Drama of Worship

What, then, are the basic key metaphors or concepts underlying the image of God's governance that we are to rehearse in the drama of worship? Biblical governance symbolism is rooted in a covenant whose partners are Yahweh/God, the people, and the land. We might say today that the heart of God's governance is an ecological covenant in which we are constituted and sustained as God's people.

I have already pointed out how a covenantal understanding of God's action underlies the centrality of history as a process of covenant-making, -keeping, -breaking, and -renewing. What, then, is the meaning of covenant as a pattern for governance itself? At this point I only want to note that biblical covenant, even though drawn from ancient patterns of treaty and inter-tribal affiliation, envisions a divine initiative to bring forth a creation that is founded in a love requiring free agency for the creatures in whom God's image dwells. The faithful love at the heart of the biblical understanding of relationships requires the freedom to promise as well as to rebel; the freedom to live in the truth or to lie, as in the story of Eden; the promise to steward the land as well as the power to despoil it. The ultimate victory of God thus becomes the story in which this covenantal promise is worked out among persons with real agency. In the next chapter I will take us into the key details of this covenantal model of governance in the biblical story.

The covenant that God initiates seeks to create a "people." It is a people constituted out of a group of motley tribes rooted in kinship. This people gathers in assemblies (the Hebrew *kahal*, *edah*, and later the Greek and Roman *ekklesia/ecclesia*) in which they remember God's covenant, seek its renewal, and live into its promise. This life under a teaching, a law, that transcends their biological origins is what makes them into a public reality in which they live by God's law, a law that stands even beyond the rules of kinship domination. Covenant arises in the response of a nascent people and also creates their ever-fuller reality. The way in which covenantal ideas and practices move people from the household world of kinship and tribe to the public world of assembly, argument, election, and agreement is crucial to the work of worship I am envisioning in these pages. It has been a slow movement of many centuries that requires our understanding as well as elicits our ongoing participation and commitment.

Finally, biblical covenant always includes land as a partner, whether in a passive mode as the reality that is the necessary ground for the people's flourishing or as an active agent that suffers our broken covenant with the Creator and its renewal. The land is both a "property" of our very humanity as earthlings as well as an ultimate partner in God's work of salvation. The whole creation is God's partner in covenant. Our history is caught up in the grander history of God's universe. This is the grandeur of the biblical vision of covenantal history. It is about both the governance of a people and the ordering and renewal of all creation.

These, then are the six foundation stones for my understanding of roundtable worship. The first three undergird my general understanding of worship. The second three undergird the concept of God's governance at the heart of the biblical vision of the covenantal history of all creation. Of course, there are other stones in the edifice I am constructing here. They will emerge later in the course of this brief account. At this point I want to walk us through the way our conceptions of the form and dynamics of

God's governance have shaped Christian worship historically, especially in the Euro-American world. Within this wider context we can better understand the significance of what we attempt in roundtable worship today.

2

Symbolizing Governance

The Struggle between Monarchies and Republics

How, then, did biblical writers over the centuries envision and symbolize this governance of God over all creation? What forms did their imagination of God's ultimate governance take? How did they spell out governance models that would take seriously the covenantal vision of the promissory relationship among God, the people, and their land? And how did they condense this imagination into forms of worship that would motivate, educate, and continually re-present this vision as they longed for God's completion of the divine promise of righteousness and peace? What image of governance should stand at the center of the hope and promise rehearsed in our worship?

In Israel's story of its early life the wandering liberated tribes sought to ground their common life in a law that applies directly to each tribe and individual in Israel. The promises to Abraham and Sarah to found a people led to the reception of a covenantal law, the Torah, that would order their common life. The covenant of the Torah, though given to Moses by the mysterious Yahweh who had led them out of Egypt, existed independently of Moses's will, mind, or person. Moses did not enter the promised land. The Torah, carried in its ark, did. The written expression of this Torah, this covenant, traveled around to each tribe's holy place in order that God's "glorious presence," God's *shekinah*, might preside among them and order their lives toward righteousness.

We call this governance pattern a confederation, drawing on the Latin word for covenant, *foedus*. It was a pattern of governance rooted in God's special covenant with the people but also echoed in their covenants with one another to be God's people, with their peculiar history of redemption and faith. Thus, the original form of what we call federalism (derived from *foedus*) occurred in Israel's earliest form of governance. It is a pattern in which the covenant of the Torah orders each person's life directly even as it draws the tribes into the unity of being a people. Israel was a people born in and knitted together in covenantal promises.

As a practical matter, however, the biblical texts tell us that Israel's tribes did badly with this arrangement. They did not follow Torah, they fought among themselves, and their neighbors threatened to kill them off one by one. So in chapter 8 of the first book of Samuel we read of their leaders coming to the prophet-priest Samuel asking for a king to rule over them "like the other nations." Samuel warns them against such a move, because it would alter the fundamental understanding of covenantal order by which they had tried to live. God is to rule them through the covenant alone, not through a human ruler. Even if they were to call Yahweh a "king," it would be the only king they could have. But they prevail and Samuel finds them a king—Saul—whom God's spirit anoints to lead the people. That is, Yahweh bestows the divine spirit on Saul to rule over the people. In the process, Samuel seeks to encase this king in the covenantal structure of the ancient Torah in order to guard against the usual excesses of a monarch. The king of Israel is to be bound by covenant just like anyone else in Israel. But nevertheless he would be a warrior monarch. For many in Israel this was the very image they then came to attribute to the mysterious Yahweh, the "I am" at the core of their ultimate loyalties (Psalms 5, 10, 24, etc.).

Thus begins the transfer of God's covenant relationship with Israel from one administered through a traveling law to a covenant with a monarch situated in a single center—Jerusalem—and a single dynasty—David and his son Solomon. The hierarchy of command over a warrior's army takes precedence over the equal status of all under a covenantal law. In the end, the violence of the sword surpasses the agreements reached by persuasion through conciliar covenant. The charismatic warrior-king overwhelms the priest, prophet, and elder.

God's covenantal relationship with Israel is now focused on the charismatic anointed King, most prominently on David and his successors. The covenantal bond between Yahweh and Israel, through the king, moves from being conditional ("If you keep my commandments . . . ") to an unconditional promise to David's throne (Psalms 18:50, 89:3–4, 132:11–12). Covenant is no longer primarily a system of legal obligations of a chosen people but the framework for the legitimation of a chosen monarch. The subsequent centuries of Israel's existence become an argument over the king's adherence or departure from the terms of the covenant. With David and Solomon the conditional character of the king's rule is almost eliminated by Yahweh's unconditional and everlasting promise to sustain the Davidic throne. The ancient vision of a pluralism of councils and tribes gathered in covenantal law still lives in the shadows of Israel's memory but no longer illuminates their path. Their high road of governance and hope leads through a succession of monarchies and oppressive empires.

In the two books of Kings we see the battle among various kings who claim to be the chosen leaders of the whole people of Israel. Immediately with the death of Solomon they become a people divided in civil war. All through this history, from Nathan and Elijah to Jeremiah, Isaiah, and Amos, the prophets take up the task of recalling the covenant in the face of failed kings and a fractured people. With the utter failure of kingship in Israel in its exile to Babylonia, the prophets lift up the longing to re-covenant the people in accordance with God's law. The question then remained open—would this reconstituted Israel follow the memory of David and Solomon or the memory of the ancient inter-tribal peace of the travelling covenant and the *shekina* of Yahweh? Would they reside in peace praising the heavenly king and his "anointed one" in the temple city of Jerusalem or enjoy the agrarian pastoral life in which every man would live under his own fig tree governed directly by Torah?

It was the Psalms of David and the temple of Solomon that would take center stage in the imagination of the often conflicted and dominated people of Israel. With Isaiah this image of the anointed king would become the longing for a Messiah ("anointed one") who would restore Israel as one people in a land of re-created abundance. Jeremiah's covenantal vision written "in the heart" gave way to a longing for the return of the warrior king. The Davidic throne became the vehicle of the longing for a renewed covenantal order in a new creation. The confederal memory became a footnote to an unrecoverable past. Regardless of how scholars might arrange the historical origins of these two visions of governance in Israel's history, the text places a struggle between confederation and monarchy at the heart of Israel's longing for a just order of life.

Out of this struggle, a vision of the Davidic monarchy became the frame of expectation through which Matthew and Luke, and to a much lesser extent Mark and John, came to understand the meaning of Jesus. Jesus of Nazareth had to be wrestled into the manger in Bethlehem to secure the lineage of David. His life was framed in the images of Isaiah's prophecy of a coming suffering servant Messiah who would be the true "king" of Israel's expectation. Clearly, the Gospels seek to say that Jesus's "kingship" was not of this world. In fact, they saw it as the inversion of ordinary kingship through an emphasis on servanthood, childlike faith, and self-sacrifice. Of course, all of these motifs have been used to enhance ideologies of kingship throughout the ages. But it is clear that Jesus's kingship itself, whatever it might be, was fraught with contradictions. Nevertheless, kingship became the dominant image of governance shaping the Gospel writers' effort to construct the meaning of Jesus and his Messiahship.

Regardless of the New Testament's efforts to re-construe or even subordinate the meaning of Jesus as Messiah and King, it was through the symbols of David's monarchy that the memory and meaning of Jesus gradually began to be prepared for the worship of the church in future centuries. But it was through Constantine's embrace of Christianity in the fourth century that the monarchical vision of God's governance gained its lasting dominance in Christian worship. Through the impact of this Christian worship form the longed-for Davidic Messiah became the template once again of earthly governance. Listen to the Roman historian Eusebius as he renders this flattering account about Constantine:

> . . . invested as he is with a semblance of heavenly sovereignty, he directs his gaze above, and frames his earthly government according to the pattern of that Divine original, feeling strength in its conformity to the monarchy of God . . . [1]

Here we see the way the governance symbolism of monarchy, having ascended into the realm of the sacred, descended again to shape and legitimate the rule of an earthly throne. It laid out a pattern that ran through Charlemagne's inauguration of the Holy Roman Empire in 800 down to the claims of James I to "divine right" of rule in the seventeenth century, where it came up against the Calvinist revival of biblical federation and conciliarism in the English Civil War. The Puritans and Independents, steeped in the recovery of the Old Testament and its early images of governance, laid out the framework for the recovery of republican and constitutional government that gained increasing strength throughout the eighteenth century, leading to its American expression in the Constitution of 1787.[2]

Why, then, didn't this recovery of Israel's older covenantal forms of governance gain expression in the worship of the American Christian churches living within this new frame of hard-won

---

1. From his "Oration on the Tricennalia of Constantine," quoted in Myers, *Medieval Kingship*, 25.

2. For all these developments see Everett, *God's Federal Republic*, chapter 3.

governance? If such a longing and language is so powerful and pervasive, why has it not begun to permeate the language of American worship? Why does the drama of our worship still rehearse the world of feudal and ancient monarchy? To be sure, women as well as men, not to mention people of many cultures and complexions, increasingly populate this symbolic world of worship. But this move toward inclusivity has only incidentally changed the way we imagine the structure of right political order lifted up in worship. Why are we monarchists on Sunday morning and democratic citizens the rest of the week? Why does our image of God still occupy a throne while we struggle for republics of citizen responsibility? Why do we pray for coming kingdoms when we sacrifice our lives for democracies and federal republics?[3]

To answer these questions, we need to look back at the efforts to establish a new constitutional order in the period following the American revolution. In order to undermine the legitimacy of Christian monarchy and avoid the religious wars of Christendom, the American republican experiment severed the institutional tie between governmental power and religious authority with the first amendment to the Constitution of 1787. The American constitution, and later the state constitutions, would rest solely on the public agreements of the people. Christian worship would affect them only indirectly by cultivating the visions and virtues of the Christian population. Henceforth the political eschatology of Christian worship, with its monarchical symbolization, would gradually become a private matter of personal conscience, congregational worship, and family life. The churches could retain their symbolic monarchies in worship as long as they did not seek to fashion the public order in the image of their monarchical devotion.

This privatization of worship in exchange for political peace could draw on the psychologization of monarchy already presaged

3. In a richly argued work Brian Wren called this patriarchal and monarchical language "kingafap" (King-G-d-Almighty-Father-Protector) and sought creative ways to introduce new imagery into our music in *What Language Shall I Borrow?*, 119. Ruth Duck has for many years offered extensive resources for new language in worship that is sensitive to these issues. See, for a start, her early collection, *Flames of the Spirit*.

by St. Paul's and Augustine's search for a means of self-control anchored in Christ's rule in our hearts (Romans 13:12–14). What was to be governed by the kingship of Christ was first of all one's own passions and wayward impulses. As Frances Havergal put it in the well-loved Gospel song, "Take My Life and Let it Be":

> Take my will and make it thine;
> It shall be no longer mine.
> Take my heart, it is thine own;
> It shall be thy royal throne . . .

Such individual self-control was good for republican order as well as for the accommodation between the churches and government. The internal monarchy of self-control cultivated the disciplined citizens necessary for a public life of honesty, reasonable debate, and persuasion. The covenant between God and nations was transmuted into the personal relationship of faith and fidelity between each believer and God. The covenantal habits cultivated in each person's relationship with God could then be translated into the predisposition to make and keep promises in business contracts as well as legal constitutions.

Such devotion was also a matter of the hearth as well as of the heart. The psychologization of monarchical symbolism found nurture and expression in the bourgeois Christian image of the Christian home. Emerging in the nineteenth century, the ideal of the Christian home was a structural expression of the patriarchal and monarchical order rehearsed in worship. It was in appearance a male-headed pyramid of authority disciplining the emotions of women and children just as Christ's headship of the male was supposed to discipline his passions. At the same time, because most men's power was being removed from the home to seek its way in market and mill, women slowly became the authorities of the home. Like Mary in the medieval church, they pulled the strings that kept this little church going—creating, sustaining, and redeeming it. Church and home became the realm of patriarchal monarchy in a world governed by republican constitutions and market contracts.

The most obvious symbolic expression of this accommodation was the rise of Christmas as the most celebrated Christian festival of the year. With Handel's rendition of the Messianic monarchical hope ringing in our ears, we celebrate the royal birth of a son who will ascend the throne of God's kingdom and rule in our hearts forever. That an infant son can already be hailed as king can only occur in a world of inherited monarchy. In his glow even the wise men of Matthew's gospel became kings in popular song. For all of this it is still a festival of intimacy and the private life. It is a feast of family and home, much to the benefit of the marketplace.

This, at least, was the emerging ideal for white Protestants. Other Biblical themes still echoed in the rest of American life. The call of exodus still reverberated through the worship life of the children of enslaved Africans seeking liberation from the Egypt of slavery and segregation. While this often became individualized as well, the thrust of collective aspirations always lay very near the surface, leading time and again to efforts of collective liberation for the descendants of slavery's oppression.

However, this accommodation was not without its strains. The dream of David's monarchy and patriarchal rule continually breaks out into the halls of the wider republic. There has always remained a desire to make the heaven of Christ's kingship descend to earth in literal form. Millennial visions of Christ's rule have erupted continually in American life. Images of conquest and of the realization of biblical political promises have flowed into European and American visions of empire and manifest destiny—forces that have always threatened to overturn the fragile republic for the sake of military order and victory. In the last few years Americans have seen this drive for a theocratic Christian nationalism burst into flames once again. We Americans are repeating the struggle, though in different dress, between monarchy and truly republican, covenantal order in the culture wars over gender, race, constitutionalism, and the meaning of America as a historical project.

The challenge to reconstruct Christian worship offered by the recovery of ancient conciliar and covenantal governance was put on hold during the nineteenth-century privatization of the church's worship life. The republican and democratic revolutions of the modern world could find no critical voice in the worship life of the church. The contest over the proper role of Christian worship in shaping public life calls us back to the task again of dealing in a critical manner with the images of God, Christ, and salvation history that shape our worship.

The task is two-fold. First, what would the alternative symbolism of covenantal, conciliar governance look like in Christian worship? What if our understanding of the significance of Jesus's life, death, and resurrection had been shaped by Israel's ancient covenantal longing up to the time of Samuel rather than by the search to recover the glories of David and Solomon? How should we construe Yahweh's continual renewal of the covenant of righteousness with Israel? How should we understand and practice the reconciliation of those who have broken bonds of faithfulness? How should our worship practices embody the "covenantal conversation" to which the Bible gives witness?

Second, even if Christian worship were reordered by the symbols of Israel's ancient longing, how should this affect the relation of the Christian publics, with their reconstructed symbolism, to the wider general republics in which they live? What would it mean for the pattern of word and response in worship to be pursued in the often un-civil conversations of its environing publics? What would it mean to take the principles of justice-seeking rehearsed in worship into the wider world? Most of this book will seek to respond to the first question. At the end I will turn briefly to the second, which has received considerable treatment over the years from theologians, ethicists, and political and legal theorists.

3

Covenant and Republic

Toward a Symbol of Governance

IT IS AT THIS point that people may become uncomfortable about an explicit discussion of political theory with respect to worship reform. Because our usual worship is encased in the symbolism of a form of governance out of our distant past, namely patriarchal monarchy, it appears to be "non-political." Worship matters are therefore discussed in terms of psychology, cultural anthropology, aesthetics, or literary analysis in conjunction with theology.[1] The symbols of monarchy and patriarchy remain as traditional, even nostalgic, window-dressing. We descend into arguments over music styles rather than alternative patterns of God's order of justice and peace. The connection of worship with political theory is simply forgotten. Moreover, to re-introduce

---

1. For a recent effort to directly address matters of power and authority in worship see Johnson and Wymer, eds, *Worship and Power*, esp. Johnson and Wymer, "Introduction," and Ronald Allen, "The Power to Resist Empire." James K. Smith, in his densely argued three-volume exploration of the social meaning of worship, (Smith, "Cultural Liturgies") explores many of the issues that concern me in this book, but unfortunately does not explore the questions of the symbolism of political order that I raise here. Indeed, monarchical symbols are prominent, and uncriticized, throughout these volumes.

political theory as a robust companion to worship appears as an alien task that would corrupt worship, not to mention endanger the doctrines of separation of church and state or of the purity of the church apart from matters of civil governance. It seems to reintroduce a "Constantinian" model of state churches rather than a reclaiming of the essential struggle of biblical faith that is rehearsed in our core worship as Christians and as Jews. In order to reclaim and transform this struggle for God's righteous ordering of the world, we must deal with the political and governance symbols embedded in Christian worship.

First, let us look at the key symbols and concepts that might come on stage to flesh out the ethical visions of governance rooted in the church's origins and in the hard-won ethical visions of our own time. They contain images of republics, constitutions, federalism, presidency, and democratic participation. What might these key political concepts mean?

Publics, Republics, and the Ecclesia

"Republic" is just one of the major ways of talking about the proper general order of power and authority in our world. "Democracy" and "commonwealth" also have distinguished pedigrees. I have placed the concept of republic at the center of this constellation of terms for several reasons. First, it articulates a principle of political order, as distinguished from democracy, which at its core only deals with the principle of participation. Republics are efforts to provide a structure for this widespread participation in self-government. Republics are grounded in publics, that is, assemblies of people, who come together not because of their biological similarities or kinship but because of a desire to live together and share a common land. They are united by a sense of justice grounded in equal treatment, fairness, and law rather than a sense of honor rooted in loyalties to families and individuals. This is what inevitably moved republics to sever their ties with kingship, whose principle is biological descent rather than voluntary consent. In kingdoms, either the king is descended from earlier kings or, if elected, is seen to be "kin" of the people. That is, kingship is a principle of ethnicity rather than publicity, of kinship rather than constitutional loyalty. A kingdom is a household writ large in which the ruler is the parent of the people. This is why queens can fit its frame so easily. It is a pattern of rule in which parental love and nurture are confused with justice and governance.

Although Matthew and Luke often saw Jesus through monarchical eyes, the actual experience of the early followers of his Way was quite different. The early church, with its struggle to transcend family and ethnic ties, saw itself first of all as an assembly (*ekklesia*) rooted in a common faith, hope, and mutual care. It was an assembly in which the Holy Spirit worked among the gathered believers for unity of purpose and mutual care. Its origins in the Pentecostal outbreak of the Holy Spirit broke through the alienation of linguistic diversity without obliterating the uniqueness of each tongue. It also fundamentally severed the connection of kinship to the core of faithful assembly. The rite of baptism, when it was not reduced to a mere "Christening" at birth, was the rite that changed sons and daughters into citizens of God's new city (Ephesians 2:19; Philippians 3:20). In that baptism they experienced a fundamental equality grounded in their very souls.

That is, the church's origins are rooted in a fundamental political need to form a common discourse that enables citizens to engage in the practices of persuasion—in the case of the church, an art of persuasion about the leadings of the Holy Spirit present in Christ. These early Christians tied a wide-spread longing for a more perfect public to the church's source in the Pentecostal mystery of shared understanding and discourse. Indeed, I would argue that it is at Pentecost that the resurrected Christ became actual and powerful in people's lives. Easter is the foundation for the full resurrection presence of Christ in the Spirit at Pentecost. In receiving the full presence of this Christ, the church begins to live into a new created order. In this Pentecostal outbreak, the church emerges as a peculiar public assembly that anticipates an unimaginable perfection of humanity and the whole creation.

A public is not merely a congregation of people, but of people who are "locked in argument about their common good," to use John Courtney Murray's phrase.[2] They are not merely registering their opinions in secret, whether electronically or in voting booths. They are arguing with each other, seeking to persuade one another, struggling in conversations to identify the right questions and press for greater understanding and mutual agreement. A public is composed of people speaking with each other about matters they have in common. Their speech is not only about the land and wealth they already share but about the possible futures they might have together.

The problem most churches face is that the early church's adoption of a patriarchal familial model for church organization eclipsed the Pentecostal dynamic of full publicity. The word "from above" replaced the "word among us."[3] Roundtable worship can be seen as an effort to recover the Pentecostal dynamic of this radical gift of public conversation.

Formation for Public Life: Participation, Pluralism, Equality, and Persuasion

This reclamation of the spirit of the Christian assembly also has direct implications for the public environment of the church. The church can be a place that not only rehearses the virtues necessary for public life but also experiments for ways to conduct the public conversation itself. In the writings of Paul and other early church writers we see a struggle to articulate a catalog of virtues that reconfigured the classical virtues of courage, temperance, prudence, and justice with virtues that are "fruits of the Spirit"—love, joy, peace, patience, kindness, generosity, faithfulness, gentleness, and self-control (Galatians 5:22–23). The classical public virtues were placed in an even broader context of a public longing for a more perfect "city" (as the author of the Letter to the Hebrews put it)

---

2. Murray, *We Hold These Truths*.

3. A now classic account of this development is rendered by Elisabeth Schüssler-Fiorenza in Schüssler-Fiorenza, *In Memory of Her*.

as well as a more profound spirit of common humanity upheld by God's creative power. (See Colossians, chapters 1 and 3.) The exercise of these virtues was not, as in the classical polis, a path to immortal fame, but an exercise of the spirit of a new life "in Christ" that has overcome the fear of death propelling such anxious striving. The concept of God's Republic leads us to place our inherited ideals of republican governance within the wider framework of God's purposes for a new humanity in a new creation. Both are necessary to understand our participation in present publics and in the fullness of God's Republic yet to come.

How, then, do we cultivate these virtues as emerging citizens of God's Republic? The courage to participate in public requires little rehearsals in trusting circles of friends before our entrance into the larger company of strangers. In these little publics, indeed little theaters, we seek to express who we are in a way that will find resonant confirmation. Such small group experiences, whether in the early Methodist classes, the meetings of Friends, or the *"communidades de base"* of Latin America, have been essential sources of the church's renewal throughout its history. In this sense, the church is not only an anticipatory public but also a "proto-public," generating new publics in and around it. This process of rehearsal finds its most explicit appearance in the church's worship. Roundtable worship is centered in this task of formation in conversation about reconciliation and the common good. Rather than interpret the "Word" as a one-way utterance or command, it rehearses a conversational interchange at the heart of this peculiar republic of God's spirit.

Much of who we are arises in the interaction between the roles we take on in these little performances and our own rendition of them. As narrative theologians have held, we gain our own unique persona in history through playing the roles of others who have gone before us. Our courage grows as we live into the roles of the saints. Gradually we are enabled to move to a fuller profession of who we are as a participant in the central drama of our historical communities. The assembly of Christians ought to help people enter into the widest possible drama of God's saving intention for the creation. Thus, the courage to participate in the dramas of our lives is shaped by our rehearsal of the life of a fuller republic of resonance and confirmation for which we hope in faith.

Publics are also arenas with a disconcerting variety of people. Every public not only is built on a pluralism of participants but also fosters greater pluralism as people share opinions, judgments, and perspectives. It is this very plurality that despots and dictators seek to override or extinguish for the sake of some imposed uniformity or familial conformity. In the work of a vital public people are invited, and indeed sometimes constrained, to transmute their necessary differences based in biology and origin into differences that can be argued for the sake of mutual accommodation and benefit. A robust public seeks to lead people beyond the differences they cannot change to live a life together based on the ways they can agree to live with and indeed be enriched by their differences. A public assumes the existence of conflicts and provides a stage and process for working toward their reconciliation. In worship we rehearse the foundational commitments in which this reconciliation is pursued. In a world of many forces of oppression and limitations on our flourishing, worship of this kind both empowers us in hope and forms us in patterns of action aligned with this wider purpose.

The capacity to engage this pluralism in a public way demands self-restraint and moderation as well as a prudential sense for actions appropriate in complex situations. These two classic virtues of temperance and prudence are critical ingredients in a life of persuasion that respects other citizens as well as the limits of one's own power and perceptions. They are not unrelated, then, to what some people call public friendship or public love. Here the love extolled in the Scriptures is linked to the conditions not of familial intimacy but of public life, of life in the assembly, the congregation of God's people. This is in part the meaning of the word charity, which needs to be rescued from reduction to sheer benevolence and restored to its place as a description of right relationship among people who consider themselves equal in dignity if not in actual power.

These virtues also take us back to the enduring Christian virtue of humility. Humility has two meanings: It asks us to recognize the limits of our knowledge and power, drawing us back from the arrogance and pride that destroys human mutuality. Classically, it tended to uphold a hierarchical social order in which people were to be humble before their natural superiors. However, civil humility is the recognition of our limits with regard to fellow citizens and our need to subject ourselves to the covenants and laws by which both our ancestors and our own generation have sought to live together in peace. Secondly, humility reminds us of its Latin root in *humus*, the earth. Humility asks of us constantly to recognize that we are creatures of earth and must learn to live within its powers and constraints. It asks us to recognize the creaturely citizenship of all beings as we seek to live in peace on this planet. We seek to rehearse both of these meanings within roundtable worship. It is not an easy challenge to meet.

Publics, in order to remain forums of persuasion, require the development of a rough equality among the participants. Equality, a value usually attached to the field of democratic ideas, is not a mechanical or mathematical identity among the participants. It is not a matter of their having identical strength. Rather it points to a quality of participation in the life of persuasion. That is, it flows from the kinds of relationships people have in a public. For persuasion to occur there must be some rough equality of strengths—economic, intellectual, and coercive. But the purpose of this rough equality is not to secure the isolation of each from the other in a condition of private defensiveness. It is to enable them to enter into a public life of persuasion and relationships grounded in consent concerning their common good. Indeed, it is to enable them to live a life in genuine covenants of peace.

Baptism is the singular fundamental ritual by which Christians affirm this equality. It is the mark of citizenship in the church's assembly. It affirms that our basis of participation is not the conditions of our birth but our adherence to the Spirit of Christ, who inaugurates and presides in this unique assembly. Thus, baptismal equality is not merely a claim of individual equality, but of participation in the underlying Spirit of the assembly grounded in God's reconciling work in Christ.

This baptismal equality in Christ's Spirit entails that the work of persuasion requires a common commitment to a truth that constrains us all. The greatest threat to a public's life is the flood of lies that comes from those who seek power through coercion by eliminating this common truth. It is a threat greatly amplified by the media revolutions of our own time. It is a threat Jesus recognized as he called out "the father of lies" in his own prophetic judgment (John 8:44).

At the same time, this truth is not simply a fixed revelation or scientific formula immutably shaping the discourse of this public. It is an ongoing process of continual confirmation, reconfirmation, and discovery. In the language of the early church, the Holy Spirit is continually leading the assembly into further truth (John 16:13). Truth is a leading light of continually evolving agreement in the discourse shaped by the spirit of Christ's self-giving and creative love. It is tied inextricably to the covenantal faithfulness rooted in God's ancient, unfolding promises of a new creation and a life everlasting. This is what it means to say that Jesus, as the embodied Christ, is the "truth" of our lives. It is this kind of search for Truth that we live into in the circle conversation at the heart of roundtable worship.

Publics Need Covenants

A public, or a republic, is characterized by such participation, pluralism, equality, and persuasion. It has connections to democratic ideas of equality and of a common weal. But none of these principles or activities can exist for long without the presence of some sense of common bonds, connections, and purposes. I have already sketched out the way some of the virtues of public life can be related to the theological virtues flowing from participation in the assembly that longs for the completion of God's purposes for creation. However, we still need to identify the way the relationships among the participants and among the publics they inhabit can be grounded more deeply. In order for people to argue out their agreements they have to have some things in common that can enable them to engage in the life of public argument, persuasion, cooperation, and mutual care. The commonality underlying this persuasive public is not only a fundamental set of "truths" but a core of mutual trust and commitment. In the worlds of biblical assembly and of subsequent republican life this role has usually been played by the idea of covenant.

Worship infused with anticipation of God's Republic ineluctably leads us to the symbol of covenant and its political expression in constitutionalism and federalism. Covenant as a concept of vowed relationship stands in contrast to biological bonds of family, kinship, tribe, and race. It is a set of promises oriented toward the future rather than a bond anchored in the biological givens of the past. Covenant is rooted in promise rather than paternity or maternity. It is covenant that first provides a principle of human organization beyond kinship. Covenant, originally referring to the treaties among the powers of the ancient world, emerged as the primary metaphor for understanding the relationships among Israel's tribes as well as of their relation to a source of order that transcended the ties of ancestry and descent. I want to take some time to develop this concept, since it lies at the heart of the form of worship I am developing here. It is these themes that worship needs to rehearse in its symbols and rituals.

While the abiding power of kinship almost swallowed up this principle of promise, Israel managed to steer away from a sense of kinship with the divine. The people of Israel were not sons of Yahweh but servants or partners in promise. If anything, in those patriarchal days, they were "sons (or children) of the covenant" (*b'nai b'rith*). They were not descended from God, but chosen and elected by the Holy One. They stood in a relation of political promise rather than biological necessity.

The peculiar relation of freedom and obligation in covenantal relationships can be seen in the presence of two crucial aspects of biblical covenant. On the one hand, in its primary form covenant is simply offered by God to the people as a presupposition of their existence. The people can refuse to enter into this covenant but they are not really free to change it. It comes down from above like the surrender terms offered by a suzerain to a potential vassal. Moses' reception of the Ten Commandments on Mount Sinai is its archetypal expression. On the other hand, even in the biblical account, the covenant is also the product of negotiation, including, I might add, Moses' clever chastisement and shaming of Yahweh to prevent Yahweh's destruction of Israel for its idolatry at Sinai (Exodus 32:11–14). Out of this negotiation we have different readings of this covenant in Exodus 20 and Deuteronomy 5, not to mention its elaboration in Leviticus. Covenant-making thus has two aspects. It is both presupposed (and thus imposed on the present generation) as well as negotiated among contemporaries. Covenant's implicit mutuality is rooted in its promissory character. Both sides subscribe to it as a way of securing the future. It has dimensions of remembrance as well as anticipation, both of which we try to actuate in roundtable worship.

Covenant can also be a solemn agreement among outright equals, as in the covenant between Jonathan and David (I Samuel 18:3). This idea of covenant is further democratized, so to speak, in St. John's presentation of Jesus' statement to his disciples that they should know themselves not merely as servants but as friends (John 15:15). Covenant provides a world of political freedom rooted in persuasion and promise as well as a world of cultural presuppositions rooted in received covenants.

This covenantal relationship of promise in Israel's life meant that the drama of its life was not rooted in the cycles of nature and natural necessity, but in keeping promises, in anticipating the fulfillment of promises, and in memory of the trust that emerges with the keeping of promises. Israel's life was also full of lament, confession, and repentance in the breaking of promise. The idea of covenant thus underlies Israel's dramatic sense of history as promise-making, promise-keeping, promise-breaking, and promise-restoring. This is the grand drama of salvation history that needs to underlie all forms of Christian worship.

Covenant provides the frame not only of historic drama but also of mutual obligation. The promises of God and of Israel constituted the instruction in relationship at the heart of Torah as well as the rules of life for those in covenant, both ritually and socially. This covenantal framework served as the reference point for Israel's arguments about justice and goodness. This covenant was rehearsed at Passover through ritual recitations of God's gracious calling and liberation of the tribes of Israel. It shaped and formed the virtues of justice that had to permeate their behavior and disposition if they were to be true to the kind of God who rescued them from slavery.

Covenant establishes norms of justice but does so within a framework of fidelity to God, the Covenanter. It unites the virtues of justice and faith. It was only in confidence of God's faithful protection of Israel that the citizens of Israel could be freed to pursue justice with one another and with the stranger in their midst. The collapse of justice in Israel was always connected to Israel's loss of faith in God and its anxious, fearful desire to protect itself through coercion and warfare rather than righteousness and fidelity.

Biblical covenant was not only tied to the rehearsal of right relationships among the people but between them and the land. This land was a place of habitation for the people. It created boundaries of peace—the purpose of the book of Numbers. That these boundaries of peace have also been the basis for brutal warfare over the centuries is part of the burden of our own sin that we bear in the tragedies of history. The divine intention was peace and human well-being.

However, this covenant does not simply establish Israel's rights and duties as a particular people in a particular space. For Israel as well as for us who receive this tradition, God's covenant-making also entails the care of land as a part of creation. There is an inextricable link between the keeping of covenant and the care and keeping of the land, not merely to advance our own self-interest, but also to affirm it is an expression of God's creative goodness. Creation itself is a participant in God's covenant, not only with Israel but also with all of humanity. Without this ecological move, covenant can be reduced to the legitimization of our own special claims to a piece of land, rather than the divine call to care for the land in the context of all of creation. Today, we can recognize that the covenantal heritage draws us to a mutual relationship with all creation. The other creatures of our natural world are also in some sense participants in this divinely rooted covenant. This is the ecological moment in covenantal life. This "world-house" is literally the ground of our common weal as well as history's theater.[4] Covenant is bound to creation as well as to our own longing for the perfection of our life together.

Covenant and Constitutionalism

Finally, covenant leads us ineluctably to two crucial political concepts—constitutionalism and federalism. Both are deeply indebted to the covenantal tradition. Constitutions in the republican world are the modern manifestation of covenantal promise-making. The Pentateuch itself is a kind of written constitution for the people of Israel. It established the basic agreements by which the people sought to govern themselves. In our own time constitutions define the conditions of membership, the allocation of powers and authority, and the procedures for selecting and limiting leadership and representation. While they arise from the arguments of the people's public assemblies, they also sink roots deep beneath them in order to become a stable world of reference for the ongoing governance of the people. They are both presupposed and also constantly renegotiated in the course of their history. They are not merely rooted in the spirit of the ancestors but also in the spirit of each new generation.

Thus, covenant is seen as the foundation of law in the sense that it provides the basic set of trustworthy expectations by which a people might create and engage in public life. Without such law we are reduced to caprice and coercion. It is through trust in this law that Israel secures its freedom in a chaotic world. This is why

---

4. A number of these themes are taken up in the essays in Ayre and Conradie, eds., *The Church in God's Household*.

the law is seen as such a gracious gift of liberation. Thus, Israel saw the Torah as its true king. Even today Torah scrolls often receive a crown in Jewish worship to remind people of the supremacy of God's law. In the seventeenth century the Scottish Presbyterian theologian Samuel Rutherford countered the claims of monarchy with the slogan *Lex Rex* ("The law, the king"). Governance is grounded not in personal loyalty to a ruler but in covenantal obligation to a framework of law.

Unfortunately, Christians in the Latin West have tended to see this law through the eyes of St. Paul and St. Augustine. Whether or not they understand these theologians correctly, they have come to see "law" simply as the bringer of guilt, fear, and anxiety. It is seen in its psychological impact on perfectionist personalities rather than as the political basis for a free republic. This psychologization of law and the covenantal thought behind it has thus reinforced a conception of worship as the therapeutic care of individuals rather than as the rehearsal of the covenantal grace that makes possible a free public assembly.

Covenant and Federalism

Covenantal thought and practice not only underlie the constitutions that make public life possible, they also inform the tradition of federalism by which republics might be linked together in common cause. Our word federalism comes from the Latin word *foedus*, which the Latin Bible used, along with *pactum*, to translate Hebrew covenant (*b'rith*).Publics generally have to be fairly small in order to make possible widespread participation, face-to-face persuasion, voluntary agreements, and shared liturgies of grateful remembrance and hopeful anticipation. In order to preserve the crucial characteristics of public assembly and the power of cooperation among publics, republican tradition has turned to the principles of federalism to knit publics together. The alternative to federal relationships has been empire or ceaseless warfare among lesser principalities. Empire is the monarchical principle for large-scale coordination of kingdoms. Federalism is the principle of covenantal coordination for republics.

Federalism is a system of compacts and treaties for enabling relatively independent publics to function as a unity for certain common purposes. This set of compacts is itself a constitution for their common life. Each federation, being the product of promise-making in particular historical circumstances, is slightly different. Many of the contests of our time revolve around the nature of the federal relationships that should shape the relationships of the republics and would-be republics of our world. We have seen this struggle in the American Civil War as well as more recently in South Africa, the Russian federation, the Republic of India, and in the presumptive federalism of the former Yugoslavia. Whether the name "federalism" is simply window-dressing for an empire or a centralized state, it is still recognized as the dominant legitimate means for relating diversity and unity among a people. Issues of federalism stand at the center of the major arguments over right governance in our time. They are part of the grammar of political hope that should inform any worship seeking to anticipate the coming of God's right order of governance.

To sum up, the concepts of public and covenant form the biblical foundations for the structural image of God's right order. They shape the language of what I call "covenantal publicity." Covenantal publicity is a term I use to talk about activities that seek to form publics rooted in and linked by covenants of various kinds. It includes the exercise of our own free agency as well as the form of participation in the publics that make those expressions possible. On the one hand, our efforts to build public life require covenantal relationships. On the other hand, our covenants demand the kind of freedom that arises in assemblies and councils of participation, persuasion, and promise. Without this work of the public, covenants can become ossified legalism. Without covenantal bonds, publics can decay into fissiparous argument, dissension, and disintegration. These two moments of covenantal publicity constitute a dynamic in which covenant and public life can constantly renew each other. It is a work of renewal that can find life and vision in the acts of worship I am laying out here.

The Language of Governance

For our third crucial component of this republican language we turn to the concept of governance itself. Traditional liturgy is filled with references to governance as kingship, reigns, sovereigns, dominions, and lineages of rule, even apart from gender language of patriarchy and sonship. In this monarchical world leadership and governance have usually found expression in worship in terms of devotion to a person—the Messiah, the Prince of Peace, and Christ the King among them. In kingship systems right order is bound to personal bonds between master and servant, lord and vassal. Governance occurs through a network of personal loyalty sealed in oaths. It is a system of personal covenants. Indeed, our very word sacrament simply meant in classical Latin the oath taken by soldiers to obey their superiors. This idea of sacramental oath has found expression in worship through practices of kneeling, the laying on of hands, bowing, and clasping hands together in prayer, all of which were ritual elements of oath-taking between rulers and subjects. Governance in the church, along with its liturgical expressions in ordination, simply took up these feudal patterns. The "pastoral" relationships of oversight, direction, and obedience became institutional versions of personal rule. Even today, the Pope, the most obvious manifestation of hierarchical rule among the Christian churches, takes his name from "papa." He is first of all a father to the church family.

This pattern of ritual and organizational personal rule was always limited to a degree by laws and teachings that were rooted in biblical covenant and Roman law. God's rule was not simply mirrored in the hierarchy of princes, as Eusebius said of Constantine's imperial order, but in the relation of believers to the law of God internalized in their hearts and consciences. Republican governance in the modern era arose in this tradition—"the rule of law rather than men." With the rise of republican democratic orders in the eighteenth and nineteenth century, with their focus on government according to law, the images of personal rule in worship became privatized. The personal bond between believers and God, between the children of God and their heavenly Father, became one of psychological intimacy rather than feudal governance. Instead of bowing before an awe-inspiring sovereign, Christians, especially in Protestant America, found themselves singing about walking alone with Jesus in the garden. The liturgies of personal rule that once legitimated patriarchal governance became a template for the private world of marriage, family, friendship, and the home.

Christians have generally lacked a liturgy for celebrating God's law. Jews have had the festival of Simchat Torah, in which they celebrate the giving of the Torah to Israel. In the festival of Shavuot it is celebrated as the Revelation of God. Protestants have frequently arranged their worship to focus on the Bible, but more as a rule for individuals than as the gracious covenant of God's governance for a people. Unfortunately, and even tragically, when many Christians tried to make these governance connections in America, they often tended to turn biblical faith into a support for American nationalism or global hegemony rather than a longing for God's governance for the whole creation. Thus, the American flag and patriotic rituals have become a part of many American Christians' worship. The more critical approach to the relation of faith and governance advanced by Reinhold Niebuhr and others has unfortunately tended to ignore worship altogether, assuming that it is only a motivational matter rather than a rehearsal of God's mysterious governance of the whole cosmos. It is the battery for social action but not the stage of its rehearsal.

The resulting privatization of worship symbolism, whether to integrate individuals into an overriding Christian nationalism, to motivate them to social action, or to enable them to suffer the tragedies of history, has made it difficult to relate worship to the struggle for a covenanted public life. Instead, it has tended to draw people away from the field of governance into the intimacy of personal relations.

Indeed, the history of the word "person" reflects this move from governance to intimacy. Originally, a *persona* was the mask worn by actors in order to participate in public drama. Likewise, in order to appear in a court of law, people had to have a public persona. To be a person was to be a public actor in history. In the early third century, the Latin theologian Tertullian extended this idea of a public mask to the Trinity. God's *personae* were the ways God was present and active in the drama of salvation. While such a conception was subsequently attacked because it might imply that God's inner reality was different from God's action in history, the notion of God's existence in three "persons" remained. Moreover, this "personhood" was soon swallowed up in a highly formal philosophical understanding of person that neglected its origins in drama and law entirely. "Personhood" became the rational individual "substance" of an autonomous individual. While this retained some of the components of our understanding of God's sovereignty as an exercise of absolute free will, the social and relational dimensions of personhood dropped out altogether, with devastating implications for our understanding of Trinity. We will return to this problem in the next chapter.

Over the centuries, this "personality" of a sovereign God gradually was transferred to individuals, largely because they took on God's persona in Christ through baptism. In the last two centuries, taking on the divine qualities of creativity and power, "personality" came to mean the unique creative character of each individual, especially in his or her private or economic worlds. Thus, to worship a "personal" God means for most people to worship an intimate God rather than a God who participates in a cosmic public and legal drama in three persons. The retrieval of God as person in its original sense would mean a recovery of worship and theology as articulations of the great drama of salvation history—a long and difficult process indeed.

We thus have two problems in symbolizing governance. The first revolves around the difficulty of moving from a focus on individual rulers to governance through law. The second involves the symbolization of administrators of this law. Let us turn to each in turn.

Governance: Steering by the Mind of Christ

Because of the historic Protestant, especially Lutheran, sense of an opposition between Law and Gospel, not to mention a rigid conception of legal interpretation and the frequent corruption of lawyers themselves, we need to draw on other vocabulary to symbolize the rich meanings of God's Law, especially in the context of covenantal perspectives. The traditions of Wisdom, which find expression in notions of Christ as the Logos, offer ways of grasping this original meaning. Indeed, Paul called the cross itself the "Wisdom" (Greek: *sophia*) of God (I Corinthians 1:21-25). Much recent interest in Wisdom literature has been promoted by feminists, because Wisdom (Hebrew: *hokma*) was traditionally personified as a woman.[5] She is the consort of God, the indispensable womb of creation (Proverbs 8:22-31). Through her all things are created. Indeed, in this respect, Jesus as the Logos is the feminine expression of God. What is even of more interest here is not her gender but her role in governance, which is why she is associated so deeply with Solomon's court. In that world, to govern justly was to rule according to Wisdom. Wisdom entails an administration of justice that takes into account the complex system of relationships in culture, technology, ecology, and politics. In computer terms, Wisdom is the software of existence—the basic program for governance.

In this sense worship leads us to rehearse our participation in the Wisdom of God. This is not merely a matter of cultivating the virtues that I focused on earlier in this chapter; it is also a matter of engaging all our senses so that we are attuned to appropriating our world in manifold ways, aware of the mystery of creation's complexity. It is also a matter of learning how worship can unfold

---

5. Here again the work of Elisabeth Schüssler Fiorenza is instructive. See Schüssler Fiorenza, *Wisdom Ways*. See also Newsom, Ringe, and Lapsley, eds. *Women's Bible*.

among a people not by commands from a leader but by a collective sense of what to do next. This "common sense" is gained not only through an artful intuition but also by reasonable discourse. It is rooted in the "dia-log" with the Logos, the Word, at the heart of reality, according to John's Gospel. This is what it is to be governed by the "mind of Christ." Such governance, of course, requires a deep immersion by governors in the culture of the worshippers. The capacity for governance of this kind arises when people come to share a vision, a set of ideals and values, and a comprehensive orientation to their world and to the historic drama in which they participate. This is the kind of leadership and governance that has inspired recent management theorists of corporate culture. From their perspective, leaders function best when they cultivate a corporate culture that can guide members of the organization without immediate control from above. The same can be said of an army that has to make quick decisions in the field rather than awaiting directives from sources far from the battle.

In our own time we use the idea of cybernetics to express the governance implications of public communication.[6] Coined after World War II, as information technologies began to develop, it refers to the use of information to control the functions of everything from furnaces to airplanes. Cybernetics is derived from *kybernetes*, the Greek word for helmsman, which the ancient Greeks used to talk about the principle of leadership in their assemblies. Governance is a process of steering through information more than of coercion through physical force. It helps us think about the work of governance as a way of "presiding" in processes of communication among citizens rather than through rule or domination over subjects. Our contemporary world is now totally dependent on this complex flow of information to order our daily lives and our institutions. As this cybernetic revolution has played out, whether in digitized oceans of information, robotic manufacturing and surgery, or artificial intelligence, it has overturned our

---

6. This stream of thought goes back to Deutsch, *The Nerves of Government*. This perspective influenced my own early work and found a Catholic expression in Granfield, *Ecclesial Cybernetics*.

traditional patterns of republican as well as dictatorial rule. How to discipline this revolutionary force to the needs of covenantal publicity articulated here is one of the fundamental challenges of our time. While roundtable worship cannot itself meet this challenge, it lifts up a pattern of ecclesial conversation that has to be a core response to the impacts of a cybernetic world.

A recovery of governance in terms of wisdom, mind, spirit, and Logos can help us re-present the idea of law as the means by which God seeks to govern creation. This can be augmented by renewed sensitivity to teaching and learning as the art of grasping whole systems and not just bits of information. Here we pick up the original idea of Torah as teaching. The divine ordering of our lives is not merely a matter of obedience but of dialogue with God, in which our circumstance is drawn gradually into coherence with divine purpose. With the art of teaching comes that of listening. Through silence, music, and the use of non-musical sound, we can be trained to listen in more sensitive and nuanced ways. Roundtable worship seeks to rehearse this kind of complex work of speaking and listening in conversation.

It is important to remember that in its archaic roots, the word "conversation" meant a manner of behavior or deportment appropriate for social life. It was a matter of how one conducted oneself in relationships with others according to common understandings of courtesy and civility. This behavioral meaning is worth remembering as we place this concept in the core of our approach to worship.

All of this recovery of law and wisdom helps reshape our understanding of being governed by covenant and constitution rather than personal command. Through the richness of worship we seek to be able to constitute ourselves as citizens of God's Republic, living according to divine Wisdom. This means that the Bible is not in any simple or literal sense our constitution. Rather, it is a crystallization of the founding conversations of the Jewish and Christian publics that have continued to this day. Our governance through constitution is thus intimately connected to our governance through council—another key republican concept.

Just as Yahweh was present to Israel in the assembly gathered around recitation of the Torah, so Christians know God as present in the assembly governed according to "the Spirit and Mind of Christ." The Church is the assembly where Christ's Spirit, Christ's Wisdom, presides. These assemblies, whether gathered from local communities or from the far reaches of the globe, are the popular basis for the Church. How these councils of the people are to be understood and structured is the fundamental task of ecclesiology. What is important for our purposes here is to recognize that this gathering, assembling, and conferencing makes possible the dialogues and conversations that continually re-constitute the church. It is in this spirit that St. Paul admonished the church in Corinth to "let two or three prophets speak, and let the others weigh what is said . . . so that all may learn and all be encouraged" (I Corinthians 14:29, 31).

Presidency and Governance

Finally, we come to the symbolization of the offices of governance. How do we symbolize the offices of those who administer, lead, inspire, teach, and judge? What are our contemporary analogues for the kings, princes, lords, judges, and sovereigns of monarchical culture? The figure of presidency stands at the center of this symbolic field. In one sense presidents are to councils what monarchs have been to kingdoms. But their behavior is ordered and legitimated according to different values and principles. Therefore, we must first guard against the temptation of simply replacing the word "king" with that of "president." This simply monarchizes our conception of presidency. This is a dangerous enough tendency in our own world, where every dictator wants to be called a president, such is this word's power of legitimation today. While we need to jar our ears open by referring to God in Christ as our President, we also need to dig behind the term to evoke wider symbolic meanings.

People often refer to worship leaders as presiders. They are presidents of the assembly, not in the sense of commanders and rulers but as conveners and coordinators of the worship according to its constitution. By using the verbal form "presiding" and "presider" we focus on the kind of action we are talking about. Presidency is a function within a constitutional order, not a sovereign above it. Thus, when we invoke Christ to "preside" in our assembly, we ask Christ to preside through the work and wisdom of the Holy Spirit that animates our dialogue.

The task of presidency is not merely coordination or parliamentary monitoring. To preside effectively we must seek to draw in and encourage everyone to give voice to their opinions and judgment. An effective president of an assembly is able to bring participants back to their primary common purposes, visions, covenants, and missions. The president serves the assembly's constitution, not in the sense of obeying its laws, but of helping the assembly pursue its vision and be accountable to its underlying values and purposes. Thus, presidency involves inspiration, persuasion, and exemplary sacrifice for the sake of the constitution's ultimate aims. In this sense, a true president comes to embody both the constitution and the people who are covenanted through it. Thus, some republics, like Germany and India, separate the office of president from the daily maneuverings of parliament, precisely in order to focus on these functions. Moreover, the remaining kings and queens in functioning republics, like the United Kingdom, work best when they serve these functions rather than parade around as celebrity vestiges of a delegitimated but wealthy aristocracy.

This work of presidency can also be seen in the historic term of *episkopos*, the bishop. The *episkopos* was an overseer, a monitor, a supervisor. While the conception of the bishop's office was often separated from the presidency of councils and transformed into a monarchical mold, its ancient import, when cast in terms of presidency, helps us grasp some of these wider meanings. The churches not only ought to take up the language of republican democracy and federalism, they should also recast it in terms of their own theological reflection so that they can provide in their worship a mirror of judgment for the practices and aspirations of the republics around them.

Election

While many other elements of the language of republican governance deserve our reflection, I shall conclude this section with only one—election. Election is both richly biblical (God "elected" Israel to be a people) and political (we elect presidents and representatives for fixed terms). A republican turn in worship symbolism would introduce not merely the language of constitution, council, and presidency, but that of election as well. But how can we speak of election with regard to God? It would seem especially offensive to speak of our electing the Creator of the universe. Obviously, the idea of election, like that of presidency, would need some reworking.

We can begin by noting that kingship poses equally difficult symbolic problems as does democratic election with regard to God or Christ. Since the time of the Psalms we, both Jews and then Christians, have spoken of God in monarchical terms—Handel's "Hallelujah Chorus" being only its most egregious expression in Christian worship. Yet kings were either elected by councils (Saul, for instance), were descended from kings themselves (Solomon), or took their thrones by force. Yet surely, in some strict sense, the Holy One is neither chosen by us nor is descended from a parent. Neither does the Creator rule humans by sheer coercion and necessity. In the last case, rule by coercion would either eliminate the meaning of the idea of moral responsibility or imply that the one good God causes sin—the classic dilemma of theodicies ancient and modern. Thus, we see that kingship language for God is decidedly metaphorical and problematic, though we often cling to it as a veritable signifier of the divine.

Similarly, while election needs to be seen as a metaphor, it is a very revealing one. Ancient Israel knew that there were many gods. The god Yahweh asked for Israel's decision to follow him. Israel saw itself as elected by Yahweh but also called to elect Yahweh as their god as well. Similarly, much later, Christians came to claim that this God, whom Israel had come to equate with the Creator of the universe and of all nations, was willing to sacrifice "himself" in the form of his "son" (the metaphorical model nearly implodes here) in order to elicit the faith of people. In the Pauline theology, which knows nothing of the birth of Jesus as a dynastic heir, God "elects" or "adopts" Jesus to be the *Christos*, the Messiah. Likewise, all peoples are called to choose this Christ as the center of their loyalty. In this political sense, which stands at the core of the tradition, we do indeed elect our God. Election is a reciprocal process of governance constructed in covenantal mutuality.

Election therefore is always related both to call and to covenant. God calls us to elect the divine way—pleading, persuading, hounding, and sacrificing to this end. In the process of this mutual election we are drawn into covenant with the divine. We choose, commit, pledge, and promise to pursue this particular pattern of relationships with the divine. We enter into covenant.

Similar dynamics, we might add, occur in presidential elections, especially in the United States and other presidential systems. Election is a process in which we try to set forth an image of who we are as a people. What are our central values? What vision are we seeking to follow? What are our gods? Such symbolic concerns easily override the pragmatic functions of governance. That is because election is not merely the selection of individuals to perform services but it is also a statement about the covenants and callings that define our common existence. So it is with our election of God. So it is with God's election of us. They are the two hands of a covenantal bond.

We have now explored some of the key features of a long heritage of constitutional, republican order in light of our desire to renovate worship so that it speaks once again in a political tongue that can critically engage our actual practices and commitments. Central to this field of concepts and symbols are those of publicity and covenant. Covenantal publicity emerges in councils and constitutions where the work of presidency is crucial. Each of these terms can be seen to engage not only our received traditions but also our present political and religious practices in ways that alter our understanding of both.

At several points in our journey through the long engagement between worship and visions of governance, we have touched on ways that the symbolic drama of our worship is shaped by our image of God and reshapes that image in turn. Indeed, all worship is an engagement, a conversation, an argument with the One who grounds and transcends the creation in which we live. It is therefore very important to lift up how the perspective on worship that I am developing here is grounded in a particular understanding of God as known in Christian theological tradition. To that end we have to ask what is the meaning of "Trinity" in the context of this approach to worship?

4

Governance in the Image of the Triune God

IN THE PREVIOUS CHAPTER I described the way ancient Israel sought to constitute itself in a system of just governance through confederation and then kingship. Covenant ideas and practices provided the framework for visions of governance that would knit the tribes of Israel together in mutual responsibility. Biblical covenant knits together God, the people, and the land in patterns of mutual promise. In this covenant, land as a partner to God's covenant has many rich meanings that can be extended to the whole of creation. Biblical covenant binds together a people with the whole creation in the search for right relation with God and each other.

Our next task is to address the difficult question of what is meant by this God who brings people together in covenant and forms a public order in which humans and the creation can flourish. For Israel, this God was so mysterious and transcendent they could only refer to him/her/it with the breath-like utterance "Yahweh" (YHWH), the "I am." As Christians wrestled with the image of a God who was present not only in Israel's life but in Jesus of Nazareth, in his risen life, and in the church, they began to develop a conception of Trinity that has shaped Christian theology from its earliest days. While the tortured history of Christian conceptions of Trinity is mind-numbingly complex, I want to point out the path I have taken, along with many others, to ground worship in a particular vision of God as Trinity.

The Christian teaching that God is to be known as a Trinity of "persons" began early in the Church's life.[1] It was lodged most strongly in baptismal formulas invoking the "Father, Son, and Holy Spirit" and in other cultic hymns, blessings, and greetings. It also, from early on, became a way to speak theologically of the connection among creation, Israel's experience of faith, the life, death, and resurrection of Jesus as the Christ, and the work of the Spirit pervading the Christian community. All of this needed to be envisioned as the work of the same God. It should be no surprise that the path to agreement about the meaning of this complex term would not be easy. The early councils of the church struggled mightily to fashion some agreement about this formula.

This trinitarian conversation (or argument) is important for our contemporary debates because how we approach this complex image of God shapes not only our worship patterns but their impact on our actions and institutions. This is a very difficult task. First, we have to open up how our image of Trinity shapes our conceptions of power and authority. And then we have to articulate the relationships among these "persons" in the establishment of power, authority, and governance. These relationships in turn shape our vision of governance that lies at the heart of worship. There are many other historical and theological issues surrounding this teaching, but these are the matters that will concern us here.

I have already pointed out how Tertullian's introduction of the concept of "persona" through which to understand the Father, Son, and Spirit set the foundation for Latin arguments concerning Trinity. It was a view of the divine "persons" originally grounded in drama, law, and history. The Greek-speaking world, on the other hand, drew on the philosophical language of "*ousia*," what

---

1. I have found Lacugna, *God for Us*, especially helpful as an introduction to this history with an eye to the concept of the "social" trinity I will develop here.

the Latins would call *substantia*, "substance," to speak of God's instantiation in the "hypostases" of Father, Son, and Spirit. This was a language of metaphysics and natural science that is far removed from our present conceptions. The two language worlds could never be perfectly accommodated to each other, fueling endless debates and misunderstandings, not least of which was the way the "persons" of the Trinity came to be seen as individual rational substances rather than actors in a dramatic engagement. I want to hold us to the word's origin in drama and law because it is much more helpful for grasping the biblical thought world out of which the early church arose, namely one of action, history, and Israel's ongoing lawsuit over its broken covenant with God. This affinity to a historical frame of meaning fits better with the role of memory and eschatological longing that infuses the life of both Israel and the church. The dramatic origins of "person" also makes it more available to the dramatic forms at the heart of worship, not to mention the dynamics of public life.

Once settling on the meaning of person we encounter the question of the metaphorical "persons" of Father and Son that anchor the historical image of Trinity. This is not merely a question of whether we should attach our gender categories to the divine mystery but also of what governance models should be associated with these gendered roles. It is not just a question of family relations but of models of governance. The Father-Son language comes from Jesus's unusual language about his father as "Abba" ("daddy"), which is then tied immediately to his own role as son. The Old Testament has some father as well as mother images for a God who cares for Israel, his "son." (See, for instance, Hosea 11:1.) Jesus, as Messiah, takes on the mantle of Israel's sonship. He is the one who comes at the end time as the "Son of Man" to save not only Israel but the whole world. It is important to remember here that in the ancient and biblical world sonship was not merely a matter of biological descent but of legitimate rule. Being a son in a world of rule based on patriarchal lineage meant first of all a claim to political legitimacy, whether in Israel or in Rome. It did not connote the kinds of intimate care that we associate with it today or even that Jesus seems to have meant in speaking of "Abba."

But now the metaphorical scheme of sonship introduces its own problems. The ancient world assumed that procreation was a matter of the father's introduction of his "seed" into the womb of the mother, who was not a co-creator of the new human being. She was only his or her incubator. This mistaken biological view lies at the heart of all justifications for the woman's lesser role in creation and all of life. Moreover, the Father-Son imagery inevitably introduces a subordination within God's Triune life. It is not easily disposed of by saying that the "Son" is "begotten, not made" by the Father. Such a philosophical maneuver might have satisfied Constantine's bishops at Nicaea in the fourth century, but it cannot overcome the power of the metaphorical scheme itself. The very language disposes us to some kind of hierarchical, pyramidal image of Trinity, because this is how that imagery functioned for thousands of years in human civilization. As an image of governance as well as authority and power, this pyramidal image receives the metaphors of patriarchal rule and shapes them into powerful symbols of God "himself." The drama of the divine trinitarian life becomes the drama of male succession in the patriarchal monarchies of the world. In that world male succession and patriarchal rule is the ground of authority for the whole realm.

The Father-Son language for Trinity then inevitably reduced the Holy Spirit to being simply the relationship of legitimate succession (and rule) between Father and Son. For several centuries both Eastern and Western churches could proclaim that the Spirit "proceeds" from the Father. It ("she"?) is an outpouring of the divine love at the heart of the Creator, seen as "Father." Then the Western church, beginning around the tenth century, began saying that the Spirit proceeds from both the Father and the Son (Latin: *filioque*). This seemingly innocuous development served to further subordinate the Spirit, not only to the Father, who is Creator of heaven and earth, but to the Son, whose body is the church. The Spirit, in this imagery, fell under the church's control. It was to serve and vivify the church, not create, constitute, and renew it. What was being developed here was the pattern for legitimating government and church that was to prevail in the church for a thousand years, at least in the West. In this pattern the Father governs over the created order of family and rulers, and the Son rules over the church. God is in some sense a father-son pair—the classical image of governance and succession. Both are served by the Spirit that they generate, which is seen as the expression of their creative and governing power, rather than vice-versa. The Holy Spirit, like women in the ancient biological scheme, was merely a vehicle for the creative work of the Father and Son.[2]

This pyramidal Trinity led to two features of our worship. One was the marginalization of the Holy Spirit to the experience of individuals. This was the non-institutional world of mystical experience, of spirituality, and of regular outbursts of ecstatic resistance led by charismatic individuals against the existing authorities of church and state. These would either be crushed, as were the "enthusiasts" of the sixteenth century by Luther's princes, or domesticated into patterns of personal devotion. In either case this work of the Spirit could not become the primary mode of authority for a different institutional conception of the church. "Spirit," with its fluidity and unpredictability, had no structure that could compete with the hierarchy of patriarchal governance and generativity. It could not develop into an ecclesiology, much less a principle of civil governance, grounded in the work of the Spirit as such. Unlike the testimony of Acts 2, the Holy Spirit was not seen as creating the church. It only animated a pre-existing corporate structure based on father-son rule.

The second outcome of this pyramidal image was to ground the doctrine of atonement in a hierarchy of honor or retribution, a teaching associated with Anselm, Archbishop of Canterbury, in the eleventh century. The dynamic within the Godhead was seen as a hierarchy of obedient devotion between the Son and the Father.

---

2. For a fuller elaboration of this development see Moltmann, *The Spirit of Life*, and Müller-Fahrenholz, *God's Spirit*. For the relation between images of God and political order, the work by Stackhouse, *Ethics and the Urban Ethos*, is very instructive.

This replication of the widespread hierarchy of feudal, patriarchal, and monarchical power could operate in two ways. In Anselm's view it demanded that the son "honor" the dignity and glory of the father. God's pre-eminent dignity had to be restored by some act of restoration by the defendant. When cast into the framework of retributive justice, this hierarchy dramatized the need to pay a debt owed by the defendant to the higher authorities representing the society. In this dramatic scenario Jesus was portrayed as "taking on the sins [debts] of the world," by sacrificing himself to pay the debt for our sins. It is hard to overestimate the impact of these two dramatic scripts of atonement on subsequent centuries of piety and church order, not to mention jurisprudence. At its theological heart lay the image of the pyramidal Trinity, in which the Holy Spirit only played an "animating," relational role.[3]

This pyramid of patriarchal domination was not just a matter of male domination over women but also of free men over enslaved people. The hierarchy of honor and status was mirrored in a view of society as a hierarchy of castes that is grounded in biology as much as in gender. The later slavery-based plantation in the Americas was often presented as a "family" dominated by the white master in a relation of noblesse oblige at best and physical brutality and rape at worst. The biologically based categories of Father and Son not only mirrored a society based on fathers' authority over sons (and those below them) but also became a powerful symbol that reinforced the biologically based governance models of patriarchal society.

In seeking to move beyond the retributive justice associated with the pyramidal form of Trinity, we must not overlook the immense power of this model in church and society for two millennia. It is a model that has formed people's innermost psychology as well as the processes of courts, governments, and social institutions, especially those of the family. Its power lies in its appeal to revenge and fear. The desire for revenge is grounded not only in

---

3. Richard Rohr has elaborated on this work of the Holy Spirit, reconciliation, and restoration in many writings. See Rohr, *Dancing Standing Still* and *The Divine Dance*.

our love for those people or property that have been injured, but also in a basic sense of justice as fairness. That is, fairness requires that evil deeds should be balanced and righted with comparable deeds that burden the wrongdoer ("talion" justice). The hierarchies of honor and submission are grounded in fear of the unbound power of those "above" us as well as the fear of unbounded social disorder and chaos if we upset the "natural" hierarchy of society and creation. However, neither fear nor revenge can create a beloved community that calls us into ever-expanding circles of love and trust. It cannot build the community that actually reflects the dynamic of divine creativity we are unfolding here. It provides no place for the re-creative energy of the Holy Spirit in creating communities grounded in the power of public profession and expanding covenantal relationships.[4]

The pyramidal Trinity, with its framework of honor and retributive justice, was a powerful symbol that shaped the models of governance in Christian worship and provided legitimation for the political systems in which the church lived. However, the rise of republics and constitutional federalism in the late Middle Ages supplied alternative metaphors of governance, some of which were derived from other strands in biblical tradition. The democratic impulse and the drive for public participation began to upend not only family order but the oppressive orders of slavery, economic bondage, and Euro-American imperialism. Prominent among the roots of this revolution in the culture of governance were the covenantal visions of ancient Israel and the spirited assembly of the early church. However, this long revolution in concepts, practices, and symbols of governance has reshaped our worship in only fitful and marginal ways. The circle worship of our Roundtable seeks to lift up symbolic practices at the heart of this alternative tradition of covenanted assembly in the power of the Holy Spirit.

This re-emergent minority tradition has two features we need to examine here. The first is the "social" vision of the Trinity. The second is the notion of an "assembly in the Spirit," which

---

4. For just one of the many thorough-going treatments of this move to restorative justice see Marshall, *Beyond Retribution*.

displays fundamental patterns of communication necessary to the existence and vitality of a genuine public. The first is a theological vision, the second an ecclesiological one.

The vision of a social Trinity draws on traditions in the Eastern church that speak of the "procession" of the persons of the Trinity. The persons of the Trinity form a kind of dance rather than a drama of hierarchical obedience. The icon by Andrei Rublev is the most famous depiction of this vision.[5] Here the persons of the Trinity engage each other around the table as somewhat androgynous forms reaching out to one another in communal conversation.

In the Western church this social image is rooted more in mystical strains of spirituality but has been given robust support in the process theology drawing on the philosophy of Alfred North Whitehead and the theological use of this perspective by Charles Hartshorne, John Cobb, Jr., Marjorie Suchocki and others. It is impossible here to rehearse the enormous work of reconceptualization led by Jürgen Moltmann, Geiko Müller-Fahrenholz, and Michael Welker, in Germany, American process theologians like Charles Hartshorne and John Cobb, and with them feminist theologians like Sally McFague, Rosemary Radford Ruether, Catherine Mowry LaCugna, Sandra Schneiders, and Elizabeth Johnson. Richard Rohr has laid out a similar vision, drawing on his Franciscan tradition. Each of these has contributed distinctive perspectives to the work of reconceptualizing the Holy Spirit and the Trinity.[6]

At the heart of a social process view of Trinity is the understanding that what we call "God" is a dynamic process of continual creation and recreation. God, rather than being a static and eternal fixity, is the Spirit of continual re-creation in which the past

---

5. Rublev's "The Trinity," also called "The Hospitality of Abraham," was painted in the early 15th century. In a classical theological move, it draws on the image of the three angels who visited Abraham at Mamre (Genesis 18:1-15) to portray the Trinity.

6. See Hartshorne, *The Divine Relativity*; Cobb, *Process Theology as Political Theology*; Suchocki, *God, Christ, Church*; Welker, *God the Spirit*; McFague, *Models of God*; Ruether, *Gaia and God*; Schneiders, *Women and the Word*; and Johnson, *She Who Is*.

is never lost but always taken up and transformed into God's ever-new creative work. Rather than the hierarchical and static governance of monarchical domination, God is better conceived as the electromagnetic energy field constituting all reality but continually transcending it in new creativity. Lest we be misled by the cold technical language of physics about electromagnetic fields, we need to see that this very magnetic attraction is at the heart of love. The faithful bonding of deep love is mirrored in a world of magnetic power and energy. This is a kind of theological imagination that re-connects the personal, the historical, and the cosmic in a way very different from the traditional theology that drew on Greco-Roman ideas of eternal fixity and invulnerability, not to mention the biology of human generation. Just as we can no longer speak of an atom as an irreducible "thing," so God can no longer be imagined as a "thing" living in isolation.

It is important to note, as Geiko Müller-Fahrenholz argues, that the Spirit we associate with the New Testament's Pentecostal appearance is the same spirit that is the breath, the *ruach*, at the beginning of all creation.[7] The light of the "big bang" with which the universe "begins" is also the power of love and differentiation that we find in the dynamic of the trinitarian God. In this unifying conception of creative spirit we leave behind the pyramid of domination for the circle of dynamic process. In the twentieth century Pierre Teilhard de Chardin, SJ, took the process of evolution and elaborated it theologically as an evolution of consciousness toward an ultimate "Omega point" of union with God.[8] More recently, Brian Swimme and Thomas Berry have developed a conception of a "universe story" tracing the divine work from the Big Bang to the unimaginable creative purposes of God's creative work.[9] These perspectives open up new ways to understand the dynamics of public life and governance at the heart of history. They provide new templates for telling the story of God's creative

---

7. Müller-Fahrenholz, *God's Spirit*, 3, 9-14.
8. Teilhard de Chardin, *The Phenomenon of Man*.
9. Swimme and Berry, *The Universe Story*.

and redemptive action. In this, they have direct implications for our practice of worship.

In this dynamic of social, historical, and cosmic process we find a very different conception of sovereign authority. It is not the simple monarchy of the pyramidal Trinity, but one in which ultimate power and authority are differentiated in order to constitute the very dynamism of the one God. It is this conception of internal distinction at the heart of living authority that parallels the kind of separation of powers that emerges in republican constitutional thought. It is this unity in plurality which provides the gyroscope, so to speak, not only for political but also for cosmic order. It is a vision of Trinity in which the Holy Spirit plays a central role in a way that it did not in the pyramidal, patriarchal vision. Indeed, Spirit unlocks the heart of Trinity in a way that replaces the earlier image of the Father as the Creator, the Maker of all things, indeed the Godhead itself. (Indeed, our language fails us here, as it usually does in theological matters.)

This is just a snapshot of the substantially different image of God as Trinity that has emerged in the last century of process, feminist, liberation, and ecological theology. Along with this image of God we also see two very important accompanying emphases. Both of these are grounded in the importance of the Pentecostal event constituting the new assembly in Christ's Spirit as recorded in Acts 2 and reflected in numerous other passages in the New Testament. First, in overcoming the governance images embedded in the Father-Son dyad, the social Trinity transcends all distinctions of sex, gender, language, race, ethnicity, and all the other customary divisions among human beings. The work of the Spirit overcomes the divisions of Babel, even as it begins the re-creation of the world. This goes beyond the usual invocation that we are all children of the one Father. Indeed, we go from familial and gendered identities rooted in our biological origins to an identity as citizens of a completely new egalitarian public. We claim our status as agents in the drama of our ultimate destiny. We enter into a fullness of ecclesia, of assembly, that goes well beyond the experience of Athenians, Romans, and ancient Jews alike. This is at the heart of the transformation that occurs in the baptismal waters that mirror the waters of creation itself. Baptism is the entry not only into the little republic of the church but into the coming great republic of God's governance in all creation.

To speak of God's "great Republic" is, of course, quite jarring for most ears, since we have so easily spoken for centuries of the "Kingdom of God" without a thought for actual political meaning, whether for human relationships or for the whole creation. The philosopher William James opened the way for us to think of the universe more pluralistically.[10] It is not a construction of isolated building blocks with static connections but a thoroughly relational activity whose members have agency in some sense. This vision of the universe as more a republic than a machine or hierarchical great chain of being has then been vigorously developed in process theology, where the life, development, and organization of the universe and not just its human aspect can be seen as a kind of republic governed by God's enlivening purpose. It is this conception of God, humanity, and universe that seeks to be nurtured in the conversation of roundtable worship.

This utterly new assembly in the Spirit is grounded in a communication dynamic that reflects the deeper trinitarian energy field of loving attraction and continual transformation. It is in this new pattern of reconciling communication that we find an expression of the reconciling work of Christ. This new kind of public in which all can participate, all can speak and be understood, and in which all can share of what they have received draws on our existing governance notions but goes far beyond them as well. The church as ecclesia is indeed a new creation pressing for a fulfilment beyond the conditions of our fragile world and our own self-destructive impulses.

Another image for looking at this process is to claim that the Easter body of the risen Christ is in some sense the ecclesial body of the Pentecostal assembly. This post-resurrection ecclesial Body of Christ is animated by the very Spirit that was in the person of Jesus. In this sense, the resurrection is fully realized and revealed at

---

10. James, *A Pluralistic Universe*, 145.

Pentecost. Indeed, you might say that it is in the Pentecost experience that the followers of Jesus truly realized what it meant to say that Jesus had been raised as the Christ, the Messiah, the inaugurator of the new age of justice and peace. The historical body of Christ becomes an ecclesial body gathered at the table, partaking of the food that arises from the good earth and the seas. The historical, ecclesial, resurrection, and eucharistic "Bodies" of Christ appear in the power of this new assembly that anticipates the healing of human alienation and earthly destruction.

This leads us to a final point. This new assembly in the Spirit is a foretaste of the transformation of all creation that is anticipated in Isaiah, Joel, and other prophets and then reiterated in the vision of John of Patmos in the Book of Revelation. The new republic in the Spirit, as I put it here, is also the earnest of a new creation. In the classical formulations of the Church, the new assembly lives between the now and the not yet. It is always a people of "the Way." This completes the ecological vision of a new "house" (*oikos*) for all creatures emerging from God's creative Spirit. This is the climax of the historical drama of salvation history which is to be rehearsed in our daily, weekly, and yearly worship.

5

Worship in the Covenanted Public of Christ's Spirit

I HAVE NOW REVIEWED the argument lifting up the governance images embedded in biblical history as well as the broadly republican, democratic, and constitutional vision of governance rooted in the Bible as well as Euro-American political thought. Since World War II it has become part of a global conversation, with even more longing for covenantal bonds amidst our pluralism than ever before. The vision of a public assembly embracing our diversity, stretching back to Israel's origins, has always required a covenantal template whose partners are God, the people, and the land. Through covenant-making, people not only weave a common language of mutual promise holding them together in argument and fidelity. They also knit relationships among these public assemblies in order to work in concert with others. This is the vision of a covenanted, or federal, republic. I have also traced the emergence of a social image of the Trinity that contests the patriarchal-monarchical pyramid in which trinitarian thought emerged and was preserved for many centuries. In this vision the Holy Spirit stands at the center of the divine life and the public assembly of the church. In this brief chapter I want to fill out the image of the church as a covenanted public whose worship seeks to rehearse these images of God's governance.

I begin by claiming that the church is a public assembly. It is a people called out of the privacy of their families, homes, and individual pursuits into a life together. But this is not simply a mass of individuals pursuing their own separate ends. It is a people living into roles of citizenship and governance according to the guiding "mind of Christ." They are engaged in a world of conversation, meanings, and communication that weaves together a wholly new way of being in the world, indeed of relating humanity to its wider creation. It is not a marketplace of religious services, a clinic of therapeutic remedies, or a family of insular solidarity. It is a little republic, a kind of "proto-public," that seeks to live out a vision of a wider, more ultimate republic beyond even the strictures of death and cosmic annihilation. It is constituted and governed by a covenant that is a continual effort to make visible to the world the mind and spirit of Christ.

In this image of church as a special kind of public we lift up the ways it enables us to claim our citizenship before God and each other. In baptism we are born again into a life beyond our biological and familial origins. In a world that seeks to encase us in these biological categories for our entire life, whether we are gay or straight, transgender or non-binary, American or Asian, mother or child, father or son, black, white, yellow, or red, this is a fundamental liberation into a new dimension of existence. It is life lived in "grace" rather than in the "flesh," to borrow St. Paul's categories. Through acts of confirmation, of gaining voice in song, testimony, and participation in worship, we begin to rehearse our emerging roles in a wider public life. The little theater of the church becomes the stage where we live into the larger drama of God's history. This work of publicity in the church involves both the smallest rehearsals and the largest gatherings. It is one in which we are nurtured from the isolation and loneliness of a single existence into the deepest relationships of trust, of mutual sacrifice, and mutual celebration. In this emerging greater public we experience what it is to be "out," to be "free," to be experienced and confirmed by others even as we confirm their lives in turn. This is a dynamic that we seek to rehearse in the conversations at table in roundtable worship.

At the same time, this greater publicity can fill us with awe and anxiety as we experience the fragility of the network of trust on which it rests. It is truly a public upheld by mysterious forces beyond our control. Even more, this experience of fuller publicity can in turn inflame the very self-concern, egotism, and narcissistic self-absorption from which we fled in the first place. The public light can become the flame of fame that extinguishes our selves, the idol that consumes us in the black hole of its false infinity. The ultimate republic for which we yearn is rooted in a *mysterium tremendum* that can manifest the life of the triune God as well as become distorted into an endless cavern in which we can lose our way. The great republic of our longing can become a crucible of anxiety as well as a cradle of trust unless it rests on deeper covenants of enduring faithfulness. The public requires a covenantal matrix in which to save its liberating power. It requires a constitution as well as a public world.

I have noted that publicity and a public is not enough. Our publics must have a covenantal form. This is the lesson of biblical experience as well as theological reflection. The ecclesia in which we enter into the drama of God's ultimate governance is a work of covenantal publicity. Our own emergence into public life, if it is to be a participation in the divine work of faithful loving relationship, is an entry into wider and deeper covenants with other people, with God, and with the rest of creation. Remembering covenant is a crucial part of our worship.

The biblical pattern of this covenant-making involves first of all *remembering* the journey by which we have been led into a wider freedom from a personal or collective bondage, whether it is addiction, slavery, tyranny, or a totalitarian numbing of our thought and senses. We remember the grace by which we have reached a point of establishing this new bond of trust and promise. Thus, Israel remembered its liberation from slavery at the beginning of its recitation of Yahweh's commandments (Exodus 20:2–3).

Second, covenant-making involves *claiming a future* to which we are committed, even though we cannot control its finer contours. We entrust ourselves together into a common future. With Israel it was entry into a promised land. With Christians it is the promise of a new creation governed by God.

Third, in covenant we *specify what we owe to each other*. We make promises to each other even as we vow to uphold them. It is through these promises that we bind ourselves to a common future.

Lastly, we *mark this covenant in time and in space* so that we can continually remember this web of promise regularly over the coming years. This web of covenant-making constitutes a world of meaning and communication that undergirds the possibility of public life. It is the frame of reference for public argument about our common life. Without this covenant, this constitutional order of the public disintegrates into the anarchic chaos from which it painfully emerged.

This covenantal form of the public creates the truth by which people can form a common life and occupy a common world of meaning. This truth is not some asteroid from another world but an ongoing process of consensus that emerges in memory and hope, in argument, validation, invalidation, and continual re-imagination. It is a living truth. It is embedded in the larger life of God. In John's Gospel Jesus did not say "Here is the Truth" but "I am the truth." That is, truth arises in a living conversation with this God who enters into and upholds covenant, a covenant to bring the creation to fruition and wholeness. This truth is continually rehearsed in worship and reworked in the conversations of the covenanted public. It is a truth that emerges in the leading of the Spirit of this assembly.

This means that the conversation at the heart of the public assembly is always grounded in the truth that has been received while at the same time pressing toward its constant refinement. There is no truth without the conversation, argument, hypothesizing, validating, and invalidating among the citizens of this little covenanted public. Conversely, there can be no conversation without the undergirding commonalities of the truth arising in the history of the public's experience of God's Spirit. It is in this process that the "mind" of Christ emerges to guide the assembly to its ever-deepening truth. It is always a journey imperiled by our own destructive and fearful impulses. It is a way that must continually be revitalized by the emergence of new conversations that retrieve the old and refashion them for the future.

Worship is the process by which we continually rehearse the conversations and arguments that have brought us to this point even as we experience a refiner's fire of the ways we have been led into false or destructive paths. It is the worship of what some theologians have called the pilgrim church. It is a conversation of repentance and renewal as well as anticipation and hope. It is a people walking a pathway with markers that say "This far by grace and faith" rather than displaying claims of eternally fixed propositions, creeds, or beliefs. It is a conversation in and with a living Spirit—the very life of the God who is making all things new.

This is a pattern of worship that rehearses the great story of a cosmic process of transformation led by the power of the triune God whose life is love. It presents a striking contrast to the historic emphasis of most Christian worship in the West. That worship, as I pointed out earlier, was rooted in the drama of retribution within the relationship of the "Father" and the "Son." It rehearsed the sacrificial imagery begun with Abraham and Isaac and culminated in Jesus's sacrifice on the cross. It shaped the drama of the traditional Mass as well as the sermon of an Evangelical preacher. This worship was embedded in the pyramidal conception of Trinity dominated by the Father-Son relationship, in which the Spirit was assigned a purely derivative function. The redemptive work of God was seen through the prism of retribution in a hierarchy of honor, command, obedience, rebellion, and retributive justice. This was the frame of justice and governance legitimated in worship. The weekly worship was built around this drama in miniature, with special emphasis on each individual's role in the drama of redemption. The church year began with the birth of a savior king and ran through the sacrificial redemptive acts of Holy Week, ending with Easter's celebration of the resurrection of the victorious king. Pentecost followed as an afterthought without much theological or ecclesiological elaboration, other than the claim that it is the "birth of the church."

The worship year that emerges in the perspective I am advancing here begins with a celebration of creation, both in Genesis and in John's Gospel, and leads to the Pentecostal outpouring of the Spirit in the formation of the covenanted assembly living into the transformation of the world. Indeed, one could go on to a completion of the church year with a vision of a "cosmic Christ" or the fulfilment of creation itself, as in Teilhard de Chardin's mystical vision of the "Omega point."[1] This is indeed a radical expansion and reworking of Christian worship practices. It seeks to encompass more clearly the entire salvation story from creation to the outpouring of the restoring Spirit, even to the fulfilment of God's purposes for the universe. This salvation story is grounded in a circle image of the Trinity as the dynamic of love grounded in the breath (the *ruach*, the *pneuma*) and the wisdom (the *hokma*, the *sophia*) of the Creator, Renewer, Redeemer, and Transformer of all things. It is one in which the church continually rehearses the making, breaking, and renewal of the covenants by which the Holy One sustains all life. It is a story of creation and reconciliation manifested in the conversation of the assembly of memory and hope.

The pattern of justice within this work of divine transformation takes the form of restorative justice. It seeks to place our patterns of destruction in the context of God's work of continual transformation and new creation. The process of restoration occurs within a circle of conversation that enables each person to give voice to their injury as well as their understanding of restoration. This work of restoration hinges on the forging of a new or renewed covenant through a forgiveness that releases us from the iron grip of past transgressions and failures. Yes, there is no less grief, anger, and suffering in the world. This is a different way of living into the

---

1. Teilhard de Chardin, *The Phenomenon of Man*, Bk. 4, Ch. 2. Such a conclusion for the church year would replace the recent introduction of a Feast of Christ the King.

world's healing. It is a dynamic of call and response, of expression and confirmation, of the weaving of new covenants of trust. It is a call to a table rather than an altar. It is a call to enter into a common public life of mutual accountability through the Spirit that releases us from our past to enter into a new future.

These are the foundation stones of the kind of worship we have been exploring for the past twenty years through roundtable worship. Others might call it circle worship, but for us the table, with its place for food and drink, and the round table, with its images of peace-building through negotiation among equals, seemed the appropriate image for this kind of worship.[2] Let me summarize these foundational elements before walking through the ordinary liturgy of this worship.

Roundtable worship is grounded in an understanding of worship that is a rehearsal of the great story of God's creative and saving work experienced first of all in the biblical witness. This great story is a search for right relationship among people and all the partners of creation. This right relationship has been imagined in many ways that include both human governance and cosmological order. In particular, we are trying to move from models of patriarchal monarchy and its hierarchy to those of constitutional ordering of publics through covenant and democratic participation. Movement from these hierarchical to circular models of authority and power entail, in the order of justice, a move from retribution to restoration. This move is also grounded in an emerging understanding of the trinitarian nature of God that places the Spirit of creation rather than the dyadic relation of Father and Son at the center of our theological vision. This social Trinity is mirrored in the cosmology of electromagnetic fields rather than the mechanical causation of traditional models of physical life. This trinitarian sociality also seeks embodiment in the spirited assembly of democratic participation within the covenants of constitutional order.

2. For some earlier reflections on this dynamic see the essays in Porter, ed., *Conflict and Communion*. In her path-breaking book, *Church in the Round*, Letty Russell laid out a vision of the church gathered around kitchen tables, welcome tables, round tables and other ways of being in circle in the life of the church.

In all of these acts of worship we need to reaffirm that Christian worship is truly eschatological. It places us dramatically at the threshold between the past and the dimly anticipated *eschaton* we call God's future. Without this, it is all too easy to conflate our present imaginings of governance, whether of monarchy, patriarchy, or democracy, with God's ultimate reconciling order. And this is not only a matter of "now" and "not yet." It is also a matter of how our very acts in worship, whether of the circle conversation, the eating and drinking, and the covenant recommitments, themselves offer ways of ordering our common life that escape the all too real constraints of our fear, our will to domination, and our heedless disregard of "the least of these." Christian worship has to constantly reaffirm that it is an act of radical hope as well as radical humility.

I have taken some time to construct a theological framework on these foundational convictions. They include the claim that a biblically inspired conception of worship seeks to rehearse the coming governance of God in all creation. This is an impulse that worked within the framework of patriarchal monarchy in earlier ages but which now needs to find expression in the covenantal characteristics of constitutions, the ecclesial sense of public life, and a cosmic sense of history's purpose. It contains a vision of governance that is rooted in the structure of the created order as well as in a particular trinitarian understanding of its divine source and center.

The question for every theological vision is how can particular worship forms symbolize our understandings of God's saving work in a way that enables us to rehearse the grand vision of our ultimate relationships in God. We can easily see how the rituals of kingship were echoed in the worship of medieval worship down to the royal pageants of the English monarchy today. We can see how the framework of retributive justice shaped the confessional and penitential understanding of the Eucharist as well as the revivalism of nineteenth century Protestantism. What forms might a vision of God's covenanted republic take in worship in our time? That is the question we have tried to respond to in roundtable worship.

With these foundations in view, it is time to walk through the practices of roundtable worship that we have been living into for twenty years. It is certainly not the only way people might seek to live into God's governance in our own time, but it has distinctive features to offer this effort. Indeed, this worship practice only begins the exploration of what worship might mean in the great variety of public assemblies around the world. Roundtable worship as we have developed it only offers one door into this wider task. Let's turn to it now.

6

Our Practice of Roundtable Worship

OUR ROUNDTABLE WORSHIP HAS been shaped by the themes and values I have laid out above even as it has continuously tested, expanded, and refined them. Our first gatherings took place as the storm clouds of the American invasion of Iraq were looming on our horizon in 2003. In many parts of our public life we were in desperate need for a kind of gathering that could guide us through the lies and misinformation that blinded our politics and our cultural life. At the heart of this worship was the model of circle conversation and conflict transformation. Through it we wanted to embody God's work of reconciliation and restoration in a symbolic form that would strengthen us for this work in the wider church and community. We wanted to form ourselves in this kind of work and rehearse ways we could enter into it more effectively. In this chapter I want to walk you through what has become our regular worship format and describe how it reflects the theological framework I have just laid out.

At the outset, we came together around two sets of understandings. One regarded the purpose of our worship, which reflects the kind of theological considerations I have laid out earlier. The other affirmed the basic pattern of circle conversation that lies at the heart of our gathering.[1]

Our Roundtable, like all circle processes, is grounded in a covenantal relationship. Covenants are frameworks of mutual commitments that establish a bed of trust in which to live and deal with our conflicts as well as our common visions. Some of these are implicit. We only realize they are there when we break them. They are like a grammar for living. Others are explicit because we know there are alternative ways of living. So we need to put these commitments into words. Here are the covenantal commitments we have agreed on to guide our worship at Roundtable.

The Roundtable gatherings seek to provide an opportunity:

- for people to bring their concerns about their life and world to the table in a prayerful, structured conversation that respects a variety of points of view. Priority is given to public matters crying out for reconciliation. Exchange of concerns and perspectives can focus on a single topic, art piece or performance, scripture, or reading.
- for people to celebrate Christ's presence at table with tangible symbols of the bountiful banquet still to come.
- for people to worship in a way that seeks to

  use gender-inclusive language respecting the equality of all people and the mystery of the Holy One who includes and transcends all gender distinctions and sexual orientations;

  be circular and participatory, with shared leadership;

  use silence, the arts, and symbols that go beyond the spoken word.

---

1. For an introduction to the literature of circle conversation and restorative justice see Lederach, *The Little Book of Conflict Transformation*; Pranis, *The Little Book of Circle Processes;* and Zehr, *The Little Book of Restorative Justice*. For an extensive collection from Native peoples on these processes see McCaslin, ed., *Justice as Healing*. For a more general pastoral discussion of conversation in the life of a local church see Smith, *How the Body of Christ Talks*.

employ language and symbols for God's just order drawn from our contemporary political and cultural world;

celebrate the wholeness and mystery of creation, especially our call to reconciliation with the Earth;

engage the challenges of justice, restoration, social service, and care for the earth.

These commitments are clearly aspirations, ideals, and goals to guide us. They are not minimal laws for participation. They do form a perspective, a set of reference points, for our planning, deliberations, and the conduct of our gatherings.

Our second set of commitments shapes the circle conversations of our Roundtable gathering. They are the commitments underlying effective circle processes. The contemporary practice of circle conversation has been shaped by its use in judicial processes of sentencing. The various stakeholders in the outcome of a sentencing gather in circle to seek to reach a consensus that might repair the harm, to the extent possible in the circumstance, and to restore the offender to the community. Its focus is on restoration and repair rather than retribution and punishment. This practice has migrated to all sorts of conflicts, providing a paradigm for conflict transformation that at least might enable those in conflict to reach a "higher ground" of mutual accommodation. Elements of this process also emerged in the work of South Africa's Truth and Reconciliation Commission and had wide-ranging impact around the world. It is this paradigm of reconciliation, transformation, and restoration that became the framework of worship at our Roundtable.

Circle conversations rely on explicit covenants in order to pursue a path of conflict transformation and reconciliation. Each group needs to develop, adapt, and claim them for its own work. JustPeace, the United Methodist Center for Conflict Resolution, suggested this covenant for its circle groups and it is basically what we continue to follow:

- What is shared while in circle, stays in circle.
- Personal information that is shared in circle is kept confidential except when safety would be compromised.
- Speak with respect:

    Speak only when you have the talking piece.

    Speak only for yourself.

    Be specific.

    Speak in a way that encourages dialogue.

    Be brief and to the point.
- Listen with respect:

    Listen for understanding.

    Be open to be transformed.
- Stay in circle.

    Respect for the circle calls upon people to stay in circle while the circle works to find resolution to the issues raised.[2]

Clearly, a worship practice built on this circle process cannot completely fulfill the commitment to confidentiality, but it can manifest respect for the integrity of each person as they give voice to what is on their heart. In this respect we conform more to Quaker practice than to judicial practices of mediation and restoration. What is important is that our worship practice seeks to ground and form us in this ethos of the circle conversation. Let me turn now to describe and reflect upon the general sequence of our gatherings.

---

2. For a full description of this process see Porter, *The Spirit and Art of Conflict Transformation*.

We Gather at the Table

A round table is placed at the center of the sanctuary or other suitable space and we circle chairs around it. It is not an altar set against the wall—a symbol of the retributive justice exemplified in traditional appeals to sacrifice and atonement. It is a table at which we gather in baptismal equality to receive the new Spirit of restoration released into the world by the resurrected Christ. The circular table is a visible symbol of this equality. We set a candle on the table along with a plate with bread and a pitcher of juice to its side. A feather with a leather holder, a "talking piece" from the nearby Cherokee community, lies next to a brass sounding bowl. A bloom or branch, depending on the season, is usually present as a sign of earth's presence in our circle. There may be other art pieces drawing our attention to the focus of our conversation that evening. Our particular round table has a walnut inlay of crossed mandorlas in the center, laid like fish across each other. At the center is a circle of purpleheart wood that symbolizes both the dear cost by which this tradition has come down to us but also the vital self-giving at the center of our gathering.

With these objects and this setting we make some powerful statements. We are not sitting before an altar. We are gathered at table. We are not facing a pulpit above us but a table in the midst of us. We are not seated before a stage to see a show but at a table facing others ready for a meal and conversation. It is a moment calling for participation, a moment with its own anxiety and its own promise. Above all, it is a setting recalling the work of reconciliation in the Spirit's circle. By being in circle we symbolize a pattern of reconciliation based in the circle of forgiveness and communion rather than in the hierarchy of obedience and disobedience, of atonement through retribution.

"Roundtable" is not merely a description of a physical table but of a process in which all have equal voice. It takes place in a circular process of speaking and listening that accords respect and dignity to all participants. It is a conversation focused on the interests that unite as well as divide us, not the personalities that give them voice. We are not gathered around a "Word" from a preacher but in commitment to a conversation that flows among us. It is a conversation led by hope for reconciliation and negotiation of a new future together.

We place a candle on the table to remind us that there is a spirit of wisdom and illumination presiding at the table. This is a table where we declare that the Spirit and Wisdom of Christ is presiding among us. When we light the candle at the table's center we are saying that we seek a conversation in the light of Jesus's ministry and the long line of people before and after him who have walked this path and kept the light alive. In saying that Christ's Spirit presides at this table, we mean that there is a governing authority who has been, is, and will be in our midst to inspire and guide our conversations.

Finally, in saying "Christ presides at this table" we are saying that our coming to the table is an act of faith. It is a faithful trust that new understandings and new possibilities of reconciliation will emerge in our gathering. But because Christ appears in the process, indeed, that Christ is here "in the Spirit," we realize that each of us is responsible to act in accord with that spirit. It requires a discipline in each one of us to listen with a desire for understanding, to speak from the heart rather than from our defenses, and to search for a way ahead that builds community. We affirm this "Christ," this "anointed one," as the center of a peace-building spirit that presides through persuasion rather than dominating with an unreflective tradition or unspoken coercion. The presidency of Christ is, like Jeremiah's covenant, "written in our hearts," but it is realized in the crossroads of communal conversation. While we may have different thoughts and feelings about the exact meaning of the term "Christ," we join together in an effort to let this kind of spirit take root in our hearts and actions.

Indeed, this setting of the table as a signature act of the divine life goes back to the Wisdom literature that deeply informs the idea of "the Christ." A passage from Proverbs that also reappears in the Gospels gives vivid expression to this character of the Holy One:

> Wisdom has built her house,
>   she has hewn her seven pillars.
> She has slaughtered her animals, she has mixed her wine,
>   she has also set her table.
> She has sent out her female servants, she calls
>   from the highest places in the town,
> "You that are simple, turn in here!"
>   To those without sense she says,
> "Come, eat of my bread
>   and drink of the wine I have mixed.
> Lay aside immaturity, and live,
>   and walk in the way of insight."
>
> Proverbs 9:1–6 (NRSVue)

With the bread, drink, and flowering branch we establish our grounding in this earth and its fruits. Our conversation is rooted in the earth's indispensable nurture and beauty. We begin with the goodness of creation. Without the kind of awe experienced in the face of earth's intricate beauty and enormous power we lose our inspiration for living. We forget our finite place within the whole, the place of our vocation. We forget the geography of our faith. We forget the humility required of us as creatures of the humus, the earth.

In seeing these elements of grain and grape severed from their origins we also recognize our deep estrangement from this earth, its creatures, its harmonies, its abundance, and its finitude. We are reminded that the table beckons us to reconciliation with the earth as well as to each other. The two webs of human and ecological reconciliation are tied ineluctably to each other. These two pathways of reconciliation are the biggest challenges of our lives. The Cherokee people, on whose ancestral land we live and whose wisdom and struggle have influenced my later years, have the word "*duyukta*"—a right relationship of harmony among things—that seems to get at this complex shape of reconciliation. *Shalom* and *salaam* convey roughly the same thing. It is a peace grounded in right relationships among all earthly beings.

The feather—also an artifact of Cherokee culture—is a powerful symbol of right relationship in conversation. It is light and transient, yet as it is passed from person to person, it gives to them an authority to speak and to the others a profound call to listen. In our own experience the feather—which could be any "talking piece"—does more than anything else to reconnect our tongues to our hearts, discipline our impulsive chatter, and open our ears to non-anxious reception of the truths emerging from the other. It is a form of Christ's presiding in the Spirit.

We Respond to the Call

Our voices come together first in an exchange of call and response. Beginning with a call of some kind is an ancient action in Jewish, Christian, and Islamic life. It is an interruption of our normal round of activities. It breaks into our labors and our self-interested busyness. By using the call and response form we establish that this is a call to dialogue and conversation. It is a call from God, from the spirit at the heart of all creation, from the spirit that calls us to a life of reconciliation. It is acknowledgement of a movement from life-as-usual to life-at-table. To give you an idea of this dialogue, here is one call to the table we have used:

> From violent streets and shouting words
> *You lead us to your home of peace.*
> From ruined hopes and darkened roads
> *You lead us to your lighted path.*
> From the desert of our self-concern
> *You lead us to oases of your peace.*
> To your table you invite us, enemy and friend,
> *From your hand we take the bread of life.*
> <u>All</u>: We come to your table, we come to your peace.

The call can take many forms—as a word from afar, as a voice within, as a deep recognition coming into consciousness. In the ancient Greek-speaking church, "call," that is, *klesis*, was the root of *ekklesia*, the assembly. People were called out of their households of domination into an engagement as equals governed by the work of persuasion. This is the name the church took for itself as a gathering of those called out from their ordinary life into a new Way. It was rooted in a call out of our natural ways—out of gender and racial roles rooted in our biology—to a life of grace grounded in God's underlying spirit of creation. In our case this call is a call to table, to a life lived together in sharing of the earth's abundance and in conversation with others. It is a call from life in the pyramids of "natural" hierarchy to a life lived in grace grounded in the Spirit that creates us all.

The call to table is also a call to each one of us to come out of our fearful silence and find the courage (that is, the "heart") to speak what we know. Much of our speech flows from our anxiety and fear. It may sound commanding and dominating or it may sound like a croaking whisper of subservience. Both flow from fear in myriad ways. The media of our time only amplify this fear. The spirit of the table begins to permeate our senses like aroma from a banquet table. It provides a setting for a kind of grace that frees us from our fear. Little wonder that Luke begins his story of Jesus's life with the angel's declaration "Fear not."

The grace of the table is not merely a balm for fear. It is an act of moving out of isolation and silence into conviviality. Conviviality is "living together." The table symbolizes the essence of living together on this earth in a human way. The call is not an individualistic call but a call into a certain kind of relationship. The form of call for our Roundtable is already a participation in the mutuality of call and response that is at the heart of movement into conviviality, a movement into communion and conversation.

In this sense the call is rooted in God's offer of hospitality to all of us to enter into fellowship with God and one another. It is an act of fundamental acceptance and welcome. In spite of all our weakness and rebellion, we receive an offer of hospitality springing from the depths of all creation. It is not only a call to the table but to the deeper conversation with God, with the Word, with the Logos that evokes and orders all things. It is a table at which we are not only guests but also hosts, participants in the table's conversation.

The call into dialogue is not only an invitation to give utterance to our innermost concerns. It is also an invitation into a deep posture of listening. Indeed, listening and the kind of inner silence it requires is critical to any conversation. In beginning our gathering with call and response we seek to enter into this reciprocity of utterance and reception, of speech and listening.

Finally, the very word "call" always implies a movement forward, but it is a movement that never quite reaches its goal. Our actions at table only begin a process in our lives. They set a goal, a *telos*, a direction. They give shape to our deepest hopes in a tangible way. They let us taste the meal yet to come. They let us sense the purposes of the Creator who is always re-creating us and our universe. It is a sign that we are always living in the tension between the life we have lived and the life which God ultimately intends for us.

We Invoke or Confirm God's Presence

Traditionally, the prayer of invocation is a request for God's presence in our midst. At our Roundtable gathering, we come to the table because we have already heard the call of the special power present at table. We are confirming God's presence as much as we are invoking it. God is there before we come. It is not our table, but a table spread in God's Spirit. In our gathering we confirm this reality of God's continual faithful presence.

Many times after our gathering I have heard people say something like "I came without big expectations, but something stirred in the gathering and the conversation that wouldn't have happened otherwise." This is a confirmation of the holy power present in the simple act of eating and conversing at a table that honors our equal dignity. It is the power of the circle process undergirding all created things. In the words attributed to the Oglala Sioux elder Black Elk:

> Everything the Power of the World does is done in a circle. The sky is round and I have heard that the earth is round like a ball and so are all the stars. The wind, in its

greater power, whirls. Birds make their nests in circles, for theirs is the same religion as ours. The sun comes forth and goes down again in a circle. The moon does the same and both are round. Even the seasons form a great circle in their changing and always come back again to where they were. The life of a person is a circle from childhood to childhood. And so it is in everything where power moves.[3]

In this same passage Black Elk recounts how his people had power as long as they lived in circular arrangements, but when the White man forced them into boxes they lost their power and young men took much longer to mature. At Roundtable we seek to enter once again into the power of this circle of life. And so at this point we simply affirm or confirm this presence and this power. We draw out words that seek to align ourselves with the energy field of this Spirit. We seek to depart from the usual, boxed-in relationships of our work, family, and community, and live into a deeper relationship more in tune with the circle process at the heart of creation.

It is here that we begin to feel the power of the social, circular understanding of Trinity. Worship is a time of lifting up and rehearsing that which is worthy, that which is the core value sustaining our lives. The gathering in circle for conversation symbolizes this creative dynamic of the divine life at the center of our worship. The relationship patterns at the heart of creation find human expression in words of dialogue. We enter into the "Word," the *logos*, the "logic," that is the dialectical heart of God. We started with the dialogue of call and response and here we confirm its depth and power. For this communion in conversation to continue we also need to affirm trust in its power to guide us toward reconciliation rather than alienation and destruction. We acknowledge that the Spirit of the living Christ presides here at table. It does not impose its will apart from ours, but calls, persuades, and loves us into participation at this table.

---

3. Neihardt, *Black Elk Speaks*, 121.

In this dialogue we bring together the awesome creative power of atoms, solar systems, and galaxies with the personal interaction of conversation and prayer. This is what we mean by a personal God—not some supernatural being floating in the sky, but the source and initiator of a circle process of continual re-creation among actors of ultimate worth and dignity engaged in transformative conversation. The philosopher Alfred North Whitehead spoke of how what we normally call God can be seen as a presiding occasion in the midst of all the processes of life, drawing them to a more complex, novel, and in some sense complete formation. God is not simply a "cause" of things, a prime mover shoving life forward, but a presiding power that "lures" life to its further perfection.

In using the language of "presidency" and "presiding" we enter our contemporary political world, just as kingship and fatherhood reflect traditional orders of governance. In using this language we try to get at the way in which the manner of Jesus's presence evoked people's participation, provided a way of seeing and doing, and, in forgiving sin, released them to start over and over again in their struggle to live out God's purpose in their lives. In this spirit we try to link power, authority, and service. I will come back to this motif when I talk about the work of the steward at table.

Finally, to confirm that the Spirit of Jesus is presiding at this table in this particular way is to say that each one of us is called to share in this work of the circle. This is not an activity in which one or two people are putting on a show, but one in which all are called to participate in a process. No one person is representing Christ, the church, or the divine power. It is the circle of people as such that re-presents this power. This is a sacred responsibility, if you will, and we often don't feel up to it, but we gather in the hope and trust that this power will be made manifest in the formation of the circle.

Here is one example of this word of invocation and confirmation.

O Blessed, Holy One,

Preside among us at this table of your peace. In a world laid waste by our greed and fear bring the healing of your life abundant. May your spirit of forgiveness lead us to a life of thanks and praise. Open up the fist of fear into an outstretched hand of fellowship. And may the stony path beset by thorns become the meadow of your new creation. Amen. Amin. Ameyn.

We Remember

Important meals are times of remembering. Christmas, Thanksgiving, birthdays, and anniversaries are times to tell the stories that give us a sense of place and time. They remind us of where we fit into a larger drama of family, community, church, nation, and perhaps the universe itself. They help us take our respective roles in the little and large dramas that shape our lives. This work of remembering is especially important in the covenantal drama of gratitude to the One who brings us into life together as well as of the ways we have broken this covenant of being. So remembering is both a source of thanks and gratitude as well as sorrow for our brokenness. In both ways, community is first of all a product of shared memory. It is a memory that nurtures and renews us for the next leg of our journey.

Food is not merely an occasion for memory. It is a powerful vehicle of memory. Taste, like smell, is one of the deepest forms of memory, reaching back to the bright but fleeting images of childhood. Whenever I taste of peanut butter and grape jelly, I can almost feel the cold milk that went along with it. I am taken back to our kitchen. It is after school and I am eating it before going out to play basketball or softball with my friends. When I am with others in a church setting, the taste of bread and grape takes me back two thousand years, to a crowded room of fearful followers of a courageous Rabbi. Because of the deep memory contained in taste, we do not eat at this table simply to strengthen our bodies, but to enter a door into the memory of a special drama that orients our lives.

The drama these food memories take us into is one of alienation and reconciliation. That is the drama rehearsed at Roundtable. Without memory there can be no recognition of harm, no material for forgiveness, no work of reconciliation. But mere memory can also wall us into a circle of fear and retribution. South Africa's Truth and Reconciliation Commission discovered over and over again how important it was to enable victimized and traumatized people to tell the truth they knew.[4] They also discovered, as so many courtrooms reveal, how elusive an accurate memory is. They struggled with the problem of verifying the claims of people who testified, especially if they were accused of crimes and inhumane actions. At many points they had to deal with the realization that we would never know exactly what happened, what blood had seeped into the earth unacknowledged and unclaimed.

We must never give up the struggle to remember. Eating and conversing in circle is a powerful way to walk the road of memory. Remembering is a collective act. It joins personal and social life. Our action of remembering at Roundtable usually takes the form of a statement that we say together. Here is one example of our litany of remembrance:

> Jesus walked through walls of fear,
>
> Called to children in the shadows.
>
> Ate with unclean sinners, broke the laws of rank and power.
>
> At his table all were equal in their gifts and in their loss.
>
> To his banquet he invited friend and foe to share God's feast.

At Roundtable we draw on a collective memory of the original way of the table set in play by Jesus of Nazareth. In this way of the table memory must always contain an element of gratitude if it is to flower into reconciliation. To take part in a meal is to

---

4. This work has been carried on by the Institute for the Healing of Memories (https://healing-memories.org), founded by Fr. Michael Lapsley, with branches in North America and Europe, and programs around the world.

receive a good gift beyond our expectations. Many times, as with a returning soldier, prisoner, hostage, worker, or invalid, it celebrates a return to abundance from a time of privation and danger. It is a time of remembering our peril and also the gracious power by which we have survived to eat and drink with friends and family once again. It is also a time of remembering those who are no longer present with us. They have been lost to violence, disease, and aimless forgetfulness. We sense their loss vividly and we remember the contribution they made to our own lives. They, too, help nurture our life's renewal. Memory is the pedestal of gratitude as well as the stone of grief.

We Give Thanks

The expression of gratitude has always been so central to the table that it gave rise to one of the words we associate with this Christian rite—Eucharist, from the Greek word for "thankful." Literally it means "good grace" or "good charism." Indeed, we still call table blessings "grace" in many traditions. Simply put, it is an acknowledgement of our dependency on powers outside our grasp and knowledge. It is one of the most fundamental expressions of an acceptance of what is outside our power into our deepest inner self, the self of need and dependency.

Gratitude is a door into other dimensions of the work of reconciliation. It leads to openness, for it is itself an expression of being open to the support we need. This openness extends not only to hospitality for the stranger, but also to hearing and listening deeply to the stranger. We admit the stranger not only to our table but also into our consciousness. Gratitude is also a recognition of our dependence, what the philosophers might call our "contingency." We are always cradled in the arms of others, not merely at our birth but all along in life until we die. Gratitude and thanks are therefore always a sign of being in relationship. It is the mark of being vulnerable to the action of another. It is a vulnerability that requires that we trust another for our life. This may be why Meister Eckhart, the medieval mystic, said that if we had only one prayer to say, it should be "thanks." Here is one example from our gathering:

> O Holy Source of Life and Light,
>
> With beauty you invite us to the day, with beauty you release us to the night. From dark, dank soil fruit and flowers grow. In saddening tears the oceans find the formula of life. On cross and weeping women's faces we receive the leadership of love. Now at this table, bounty of your earth renews our bodies, minds, and spirits — the leadership of grace. Be here. Be now. Be here in word and nurture, leading us to peace. Be in our voices as we sing our thanks.
>
> "Thank you, God, Holy One. Thank you, God Creator, thank you, God.
>
> "Thank you, God, Holy One. Thank you, God Redeemer, thank you, God.
>
> "Thank you, God, Holy One. Thank you, God, Great Spirit, thank you, God."

As the door to reconciliation, this act of gratitude is indeed what makes this a holy time, a time that plumbs the depths of the creative life that is our origin and sustaining home. Participants may notice that we do not begin with our unworthiness and need for repentance, but with the goodness and generosity of God. There is a time to realize how far short we fall of what we can be as the creatures of a loving God, but here the order of worship begins with God's overflowing goodness and our response of gratitude.

We Eat and Drink

We then have a simple time of sharing from the bread and juice at the table—symbols of God's overflowing abundance and nurture. Indeed, as we move from this act into our conversation, people often take seconds from the table. This, too, is an acknowledgement of God's abundance. It participates in the generosity of a man who could offer bread to another man who was about to betray him. This kind of open generosity can only flow from a deep sense of sufficiency rooted in God's abundance. Thus, we don't eat as if we would never see another meal. We do not eat without serving the neighbor first. We do not eat in haste, ignoring those around us. How different is this act from the fast food culture all around us!

Some people would recognize in this act the traditional Moravian love feast or agape meal. Indeed, it is tapping into the same sensibility, just as our conversation is kin to the Quaker meeting. The table —and its conversation—has not been forgotten in Christian tradition, but its meaning has changed dramatically and varies drastically among Christians. Most of Western Latin tradition has seen in this meal a drama of sacrifice and has construed reconciliation in terms of this sacrifice. The meal became a ritual shaped by penance and the satisfaction of a retributive God. It was a reward for the worthy or the repentant. Clearly this is not what this meal is.

The identification of the symbolic meal with retributive justice and the hierarchies of church governance has led us not to speak of Roundtable as an official "Eucharist" of a formal church setting. Instead, we want to evoke the simplest core of a table gathering of nurture, gratitude, and conversation. This meal seeks the path of reconciliation in the celebration of God's abundance rather than the overcoming of our unworthiness. It puts the emphasis on the work of the Holy Spirit in the Roundtable's call to conversation. Here we see the importance of the social concept of the Trinity rather than one imprinted with the pyramid of hierarchical sacrifice. At this round table we find the grace of God's forgiveness in the power of the circle to bring us to a new level of understanding and relationship. The grace of God's nurture leads us into the grace of a holy conversation.

The Conversation

It is hard to speak of a good meal if it does not have good conversation. Sometimes meals lead us into conversations that escalate into arguments and fights, leaving food undigested and rejected.

Other times the conversation leads us past our traditional defenses into deeper layers that bond people together for a lifetime. The opportunity for conversation can arouse our anxieties as well as our hopes as we sit down with relatives, strangers, or even old adversaries. The same universe of possibilities confronts us at this Roundtable, but here we enter into a form of conversation in which we publicly acknowledge that we have stepped into a conversation governed by the spirit and wisdom of Jesus. We are entering into the power of the trinitarian God.

In conversation we bridge the gap between word and table. We are not involved in separate events of "Word" from a preacher and "Sacrament" from a priest. Here we have "word at table." The kind of word that is in conversation at table is not a one-way communication, but one aspect of the process of relationship-building through speaking and listening. It invites us all to do both. This is a major departure from our usual assumption, at least in Protestant circles, that the primary act of speech in worship is a one-way communication from pulpit to pew. This is the practice that has traditionally enveloped our understanding of "the Word." It has been this one-way word that has summoned people to confession and reconciliation with a grace from on high. In circle conversation, however, "the Word" is a dialog of speaking and listening in search of deeper mutuality. In this circle of conversation we seek to walk the path of reconciliation.

In this circle conversation we rehearse once again the fundamentals of any circle process—speaking from the heart, listening deeply and appreciatively, and seeking points of common ground to find a way together to a better place. In a regular gathering at Roundtable we usually do not come to transform a particular conflict in our short time together, any more than a traditional Mass actually re-sacrifices the historical Jesus. Transformation of a particular conflict might indeed happen, but that is not our primary intent.[5] We come to engage in a process that plants these reconciling dispositions and behaviors ever deeper into our lives. We come

---

5. This possibility is explored in the essays in Porter, ed., *Conflict and Communion*.

together to make these kinds of actions visible and public, so they might call us and others into this kind of response to the conflicts that fill our lives. Our conversation is a powerful earnest of the conversations that can lead to reconciliation in our world. At this table, our conversation has three crucial components—the readings, the talking piece, and the steward.

The Readings

Every conversation, knowingly or not, draws on earlier discourse, just as every conflict has antecedents and causes in earlier conflicts. Language itself is a vast repository of meanings, as any wordsmith will tell you. At Roundtable we begin the conversation with readings, usually one from Scripture and sometimes one from another source, that remind us of a benchmark discourse to open up our way into the focus for the day. The "word" in the reading invites our words from our experience today. We then enter into the circle of conversation that includes these founding voices.

Sometimes we ask someone in our community to visit with us to talk about their experiences in connection with some aspect of the work of reconciliation. We have had conversations on domestic violence, community mediation, prisoner and victim rehabilitation, immigration issues and many more over the years. This requires advance preparation to enable the guest to fit into our worship framework rather than to revert to a kind of public presentation to an audience. Here we have to confront boundary problems between our worship experience and the cultural customs, often non-religious, around us, especially in light of the many ways our practices of worship and communion have often excluded people from gathering at table. It is important that guests understand the nature and purpose of the Roundtable gathering ahead of time so that they feel genuinely invited and comfortable in their participation.

The Talking Piece

The feather usually serves as our talking piece, and so I will refer here to the talking piece as a feather. Others might use stones, bowls, cloth, or a Bible. As the talking piece is passed from person to person it gives to the holder authority to speak and to the others the obligation to listen, indeed, to listen deeply. As someone struggles to find words to share their experience I am reminded of the old Spiritual's lines: "Sometimes I feel like a feather in the air . . . a long way from home."

The feather asks us to speak concisely and briefly from the heart. This is not an easy discipline! Words for some are a defensive wall to ward off attack. They are a cover for their anxiety in being vulnerable to others. They cannot speak enough of them. For others they are a mist of sounds they cannot organize. Or they are the preferred means of dominating others. They are swords in the battle of life. All of us struggle with these functions of our speech. Bringing our inner life to clear, relationship-building speech is not merely something we might learn as children, but a life-long task with ever-new challenges. For some, a song, a piece of art, a dance, the tones of a flute or the beating of a drum may express more than words. These expressions, too, must be invited into the circle of conversation. The feather, as one of our members points out, is to help us "talk peace." It is a sign of our unique authority and dignity, just as it is an invitation to others to listen with appreciation and a search for understanding.

The talking piece gives powerful authorization to people to enter into the public space of the circle. This "publication" of our lives is a crucial moment in the work of covenantal publicity that I outlined earlier. Billions of people around the world have no voice, no point of entry into public life and the confirmation it can bestow. They are besieged and seduced by media celebrities but they can play no role in the drama of genuine public life. The talking piece bestows that authority by which they become to some degree authors of their own lives.

Even harder is the feather's call to listen. While others speak, it is not a time for preparing our own response. We can take a time of silence in the passing of the feather to compose our own thought. The feather is an invitation to see how the other is feeling like a feather in the air. It is a time to be hearing our tone, pace, and breathing as well as seeing body, gesture, and expression in the speech of others. It is a time for compassion—co-suffering—as well as co-celebration. We can then give expression to our own thoughts and feelings, knowing that others are also listening this way.

At this point I need to deal with the matter of "virtual presence" that was introduced into our lives during the Covid-19 pandemic from 2020 to 2022. For a while, we went into an online Zoom format that kept us in touch with one another. It kept the flame burning. But upon regaining the chance for physical co-presence we decided that we could not incorporate the screen into our worship practice. We had to be physically present to one another. We could not enable others to be fully present through a video screen. The presence in conversation had to be as real as the presence for eating and drinking.

This decision was probably also shaped by our suspicion of the impact of digital communication on our public life generally. The screen has turned us all to some extent into spectators of an artificial drama contrived and controlled by others. It has become a source of unverifiable misinformation and appeal to our passions rather than our reason, our hatreds rather than our loves. In worship it has promoted the dominance of the would-be celebrity and performer rather than the inter-relationships of a face-to-face community. These considerations also figured in our return to a fully physical circle of conversation at Roundtable.

The Steward

If anyone is called to represent the presiding spirit of Christ at the table it is the steward. While each person must take responsibility for speaking and listening, we assign one person to guide the conversation and to mark its beginning and end. I am reminded of St. Paul's claim that we are "servants of Christ and stewards of God's mysteries" (I Corinthians 4:1). In this case the "mystery" of Christ's presence occurs in the conversation of the circle at table. The steward serves the circle process. In this sense, the steward participates in the Christ-Spirit's presidency at table. The steward is responsible for calling us back to the basic covenant that governs the circle. The steward does this in several ways.

The steward begins the conversation with a statement about our focus and a question designed to open our inquiry. Through consultation in advance the steward clarifies a focus that seems to bring together the dominant concerns of the members of the gathering. The steward then formulates a question to elicit understandings from the participants. Asking the right question is indeed crucial to the power of the conversation. It is no easy task and requires thoughtful preparation.

Stewards also explain elements of the circle process to those who are participating for the first time. They also have the responsibility of holding participants to the circle's covenant. Occasionally, the steward will have to remind a speaker that the circle requires greater brevity or attention to the question at hand. This takes tact. Sometimes a hand gesture will do. Sometimes this can be a gesture to pass the feather, or a short phrase of reminder about the covenant of brevity. Perhaps it is a reminder that others need to speak. The steward also needs to give permission to people to remain silent and listening. Listening is something everyone is called to do. Speaking must follow from the promptings of the heart. The steward needs to stay tuned to this dynamic of participation. The challenge here, for the steward and for all of us, is how to identify in our inner self our prayer, our contribution, our offering for the table. The steward is one who is charged with safeguarding this process for the good of the whole.

When the talking piece has completed its round, the steward can decide whether to ask another question to follow up on the first or to lay it on the table and invite conversation on the points that have been raised. At times the steward may summarize the contributions of the participants in order to emphasize that they have been heard and to help others confirm or revise what they thought they heard.

Finally, upon sensing a point of closure, the steward signals a time for enlarging the circle of conversation in words of prayer to the listening God. Just as the conversation begins with records of founding conversations and stories, so it leads now to a wider plane that acknowledges the underlying "dia-logic" of the whole universe.

The circle conversation is an enactment, in a ritual miniature, of the underlying dynamics of covenantal publicity. It offers a way for people to act into the work of professing their lives before others, of overcoming their fear of shame and failure by holding a talking piece that gives them standing to speak from their hearts. While it is in many ways a confidential gathering, it rehearses the work of publicity we are called into in our lives. At the same time, the conversation cannot occur without commitment to an underlying covenant that builds mutual trust and that points to the wider covenants that are needed to sustain our life within the vast history of our species and our planet. Yes, these acts at table only dimly mirror the great work of entering into the divine creativity of the triune God, but they are the light by which we see that way and seek to live it out.

Prayers: The Wider Conversation

The Roundtable places circle conversation at the center of the work of reconciliation. We assume that reconciliation is at the heart of Jesus's ministry and God's purposes. It is the bedrock reality of the universe. What we call "prayer" is our effort to align ourselves with the dialogical character of God's triune reality and purposes. In doing this, however, we are aware that this action has often been reduced to magical efforts at manipulation of this reality. So much prayer seems to simply be a replication of our infantile need for parental security. It seems to be solely a petition for action beyond the laws by which we are normally bound.

Many of us cannot enter this action because it is often presented within an unbelievable theology or theory of the universe. It is simply "talking to the ceiling" or to Santa Claus.

With all of these reservations and limitations we still engage in a form of this ancient practice to affirm that there are dimensions of dialogue outside our knowledge and field of trust. It is an act of openness toward a deeper, more mysterious dialogue that sustains the universe and its trajectory toward reconciliation. It is an opening of our table conversation to the widest reaches of our circles of existence. In this sense it affirms our faith in a triune God who calls us into ever-wider covenants of mutual trust and participation in a common world. We still use words to affirm that this dialogue is a genuinely human dialogue, even though this conversation reaches beyond the bounds of ordinary human experience.

Over the years we have used a singing bowl to mark the entry into these utterances that seek to align us with the wider harmonies of the universe. The sonorous bowl, with its multiple overtones, summons us into this special time. It is a moment that quiets us as we are invited into a special phase of conversation, one more ethereal, one that strains even further against our means of articulation. The song of the bowl is not necessary to this transition. Others may find different ways to move us into the time and voice of prayer, but it has become a regular feature of our gathering.

Like the circle stewards, prayer leaders gather up concerns that have been registered at table and direct them toward the Holy One who hears and remembers all. They then ask for other prayers—of thanks, of petition, of intercession—and we respond with words appropriate to our focus for that day. Sometimes there is a silent time of listening for our inner voices, a silence that offers openings beyond our words.

The prayer leader then leads us in a "hope prayer" rooted in the form that Jesus taught his disciples in the Gospels by Matthew and Luke. Here we have tried to experiment with contemporary expressions of Jesus's ancient formula, commonly called the Lord's Prayer. In its form of address to the Holy One, in its political and social metaphors, and in its tone it seeks to embody the grounded hope this prayer form expressed in the early church. Here is our present wording for this prayer.

> O Source of Life, You alone are holy.
> Come and govern us in perfect peace.
> Give us today all the food that we need.
> Release us from sin as we release our enemies.
> Save us in the trials of judgment.
> Liberate us all from evil powers.
> Guide us in your justice, wisdom, and peace.
> Amen. Amin. Ameyn.

In Jesus's time the hope for the coming of God's governance was often expressed in the language of kingdoms and monarchs. Our contemporary expression of this form tries to open up a language underlying a different governance model. In it, God is addressed as "Source of Life." The term "Father" as the title of God the Creator is central to a patriarchal culture, but in our own time this name cannot convey that ancient combination of authority, creativity, and care as well as unrestrained power. Neither our biological nor our political understandings support it. Whereas for the ancient world family roles and governance roles were combined, we have separated them for the sake of greater political justice that respects the equality and maturity of all citizens. Here we are using "Source," but other possible titles await our exploration.

We then use language of governance rather than "will" and "kingdom" to call for the complete realization of God's purposes in this world—that is, for a new pattern of relationships among all the creatures of this earth. In the Hope Prayer we retain much of the language of English versions to express this longing for fullness of life. The terms of forgiveness in the original could be rendered as "debts," thus bringing in the sharp economic reality of our injustice toward each other and the earth. "Debts," at least, appears in different ways in both Gospel accounts (Matthew 6: 9–15 and Luke 11:2–4).

The Gospel accounts of Jesus's prayer do not contain the traditional doxological phrase "For Thine is the Kingdom . . . "

Just as it was not essential in its original form, so we have left out any effort to give voice to an equivalent praise of God's Republic, constitution, or form of governance. Instead, we acknowledge our continuing dependence on God's leadership toward that ultimate governance within God's covenant of peace.

Using contemporary words we have tried to render this affirmation of God's underlying right order in terms of guidance aligned with the imperatives of justice, wisdom, and peace. Other efforts at constructing a Hope Prayer from Jesus's model might want to be even more explicit about using words of covenant, constitution, or republic. In this way we might enter more vividly into the effort to sustain a conversation with God that nurtures God's purposes in this world—one that recalls us to God's way and renews us with God's promise.

In any event we want to remember the core message of reconciliation at its heart—gratitude, forgiveness, a sense of the holy workings of God. Jesus's prayer expresses a longing for God's liberation and justice as well as a hope for our own capacity for forgiveness and humility. It opens up an attitude toward the future that can prepare us for God's work of reconciliation. The earliest Christian gatherings at table concluded with the Aramaic phrase *"maranatha"*—"Our Lord, come"—giving voice to the hope and expectancy generated in the table experience (I Corinthians 16:22). This Hope Prayer shares in that tradition and connects it directly to the form that Jesus introduced to his followers.

Because the work of reconciliation has to include a healing of the tragic chasms of enmity that have arisen among the Abrahamic religions of Judaism, Christianity, and Islam, we conclude our prayers with the three versions of "Amen" found in those traditions—Amen, Amin, Ameyn. Other roundtable gatherings could clearly expand this affirmation of a wider community of shared memory and hope.

The traditional formulation of this prayer is incomplete in one regard important to our contemporary understanding of the full work of reconciliation—our reconciliation with God's earth. Although this is implied in a full understanding of God's shalom, it is not yet explicit, either in Jesus's formulation or in our present expressions. While future versions of the Hope Prayer might incorporate this theme, at present it is a challenge we address in our commitments.

The Commitments

In our worship gathering we move from the Hope Prayer to a recitation of our commitments as people led by this faith in God as the reconciling and creative source of all life. This is another expression of our covenanted life together. Here is our litany of commitment at this time:

> In God's love, we will seek the path of reconciliation.
> In God's power, we will walk the ways of peace.
> In God's wisdom, we will struggle for God's justice in this world.
> In God's mercy, we will seek to care for Earth, our home.

This simple statement of commitments revitalizes the covenant that we seek to follow together. It echoes the way that forgiveness and reconciliation are themselves moments in the life of constant covenant-making and renewal, along with our inevitable failure to stay on the path it sets forth. And so we need constant blessing and renewal.

The Blessing and Sending

We close in a very familiar way—with blessing and sending. It is a blessing we say or sing together. Though there are many blessings that would be appropriate, we have often used this blessing.

> Go now in peace, blessing and blessed,
> Grounded in God, healing and whole.
> Go now in peace, blessing and blessed,
> Grounded in God, filled with God's love.

At the conclusion of the blessing song, we invite participants to extend a sign of peace and reconciliation to others around the circle.

Looking back over the entire sequence of our gathering we can see that this time of communion and conversation begins with our assembly in memory and thanks, focuses in nurture and sharing from the heart, culminates in words of hope and commitment, and is sealed by a blessing. This is a classic sequence in Christian worship, but it takes on a particular content in light of our image of the triune God, of the way we understand God's work of governance and reconciliation, the centrality of the divine conversation, the intent of Jesus's life and ministry, and our understanding of the world we live in. Above all, it is unusual in placing the process of circle conversation at the heart of our gathering to rehearse God's work of reconciliation in our world.

With some alterations this pattern has remained fairly stable over these twenty years. It serves to express our fundamental understanding of reconciliation. It also serves to form in us more deeply the dispositions, attitudes, perspectives, and understandings that we need in order to transform the conflicts distorting and destroying our lives and the life of this earth. With this picture in mind I want to look at the challenges, difficulties, and possibilities we have discovered in living out this practice.

7

The Place of Roundtable Worship in the Wider Church

OUR ROUNDTABLE WORSHIP HAS developed a fairly stable form that would not be unfamiliar to many Christians, but it remains a somewhat experimental exploration in response to God's work of reconciliation among us. Our Roundtable gathering is a public expression of our understanding of God's life within and among us. It is a public means for forming us to participate in God's call to reconciliation and renewal of the earth. In taking this path in our worship life we have seen some new possibilities as well as experienced many challenges. In this section I want to lift up some of these discoveries and challenges to help inform others if they choose to set out on this path.

Of Size and Space

Our roundtable gatherings usually consist of 10 to 15 people. While they could be larger, this is a good size for a circle conversation. It enables people to participate but it is public enough that we stay focused on what is common rather than what is purely individual. It is not a setting for group therapy, though it can be healing in other ways. This is a decisive difference from worship models that are theatrical performances for thousands of people gathered in auditoriums and stadiums, whether as seekers or members. It is an expression of a church that is composed of innumerable cells guided by a common spirit and held together by a common covenant. It is a time of participation rather than performance.

Let me just pause for a moment to emphasize how decisive this difference is. Our media transmissions of performance sensationalism has caused many churches to develop forms of worship that seek to imitate the performance artistry of the rock concert, the political rally, or the opera. This is nothing new, especially in American history, with its revivals and "crusades," whether by Billy Graham or Joel Osteen. But in its focus on the celebrity performer or the show, it turns believers into spectators, even if very lively ones, rather than participants in the circle of the Spirit's reconciling work. In short, roundtable worship invites us to let go of the longing for size and showmanship for the sake of becoming participants in rehearsal for the republic of God's presence in the Holy Spirit.

The optimal shape of the space for this event is a circular or square room. Perhaps an ideal would be a domed, circular room. Indeed, the domed and circular church building goes back to the most ancient days of the church. In 2005 the Israel Antiquities Authority announced the discovery of an ancient church site near Megiddo (the plain of Armageddon). It had a table at its center over a floor with a mosaic inscription naming, in Greek, a "God-loving" woman by the name of Akeptous, who "donated this table to the God Jesus Christ in commemoration." It was later dated to around 230 CE. A mosaic of two fish was found in the floor tiles.[1]

Today, most of our church buildings are rectangular, with the focus of attention against one wall housing the stage, altar, and pulpit. It is a setting for performance and presentation, not interactive participation. Church buildings tend to be shoeboxes rather than circles. Circular worship spaces do exist, but as the

---

1. Barkat, "Prison dig reveals church . . . ." See also "Megiddo Church (Israel)."

number of participants enlarges, they usually begin to be reconfigured to put the focus to one side, where the key performers, whether preachers or musicians, are located.

At the same time, however, many traditional rectangular churches are removing their pews in order to form circular worship spaces. There are various ways congregations might partially reconfigure their rectangular and multi-level worship spaces to accommodate the circular demands of roundtable worship. In any case, a roundtable gathering needs a space that enables the group to assemble in circle around the table, to hear and see one another, and to be as undistracted from their common purpose as possible. It is useless, however, to reconfigure the space toward a circular shape if the worship still focuses on the work of the preacher or priest (or the organ and musicians!) rather than the people gathered in conversation and nurture at the table.

Here, it is now important to mention the introduction of video screens and interactive internet connections (Zoom, Skype, etc.) that have enabled millions of people to continue their connection to a worshipping community despite the separations caused by illness, disability, distance, or pandemic constraints. Video screens have little or no place at roundtable worship because of its high priority on rehearsing the dynamics of covenantal publicity through circle conversation among persons in all their bodiliness. Until we can holograph persons from afar to be virtually at table, the video screen inevitably creates a two-tier system of participation that belies the equality of participants and their invitation to eat and drink from a common table. Even worse, it rehearses a paradigm of producer-consumer dependence that undermines the participatory mutuality at the heart of the trinitarian God as well as of the circle of worship. The problem of screens and virtual presence is a vexing one that is still evolving, but under present conditions we do not see a way to be fully in circle at table with the presence of video screens.

The limited size of our gathering also affects the possible introduction of non-verbal elements in roundtable worship. Ritual movements, whether dancing and circling the table or processing in various ways, are more impressive with greater numbers and in larger spaces. While there are important rituals for the conversational scale, such as passing the talking piece, there can be other meaningful movements and actions in a larger space. How a gathering wants to balance and implement these elements will vary with the members and their sensibilities. Although the roundtable worship we have pursued places a great emphasis on verbal action, there are many other ways that people can internalize the circle processes of reconciliation. On occasion we have had meditative "walk-arounds" with art pieces in the room, leading to a conversation reflecting on their meaning. It would also be possible to have a meaningful dance with appropriate music to internalize the processes of the circle. And, as the ancients knew, the surrounding walls can present vistas of colored glass and art that can deeply inform the spirit of a gathering.

The Circle Spirit in Larger Gatherings

If more people wanted to participate in our roundtable gathering, either we would have to establish additional roundtables of the same size, thus preserving the circle conversation, or we would have to symbolize this circle dynamic in a larger setting but forgo many participatory elements of the circle process itself.[2] The first choice is, in one sense, already present in many large churches in the form of small groups for prayer and conversation. In this case there could be roundtables of ten to twenty people along with large gatherings whose form is derived from the core model. This could include sharing a common liturgical form, which I have outlined here. Much of this small-group/large-group model is already happening in churches, but without the core commitments and processes I am describing here. Providing a short summary of these principles and practices is the reason for writing this little book, which seeks to provide a common understanding of

---

2. For examples of churches committed to this kind of worship in circle visit www.rondeboschunited.org, located in Rondebosch/Cape Town, South Africa, and www.circleofmercy.org, located in Asheville, North Carolina.

what we are attempting. It is, if you will, a kind of covenantal document, but one open to continual reworking and interpretation. Through the covenants among these roundtables, we create a mirror of the federalism that seeks to preserve vibrant publics knit together for common action.

Whether or not a church has the smaller roundtables, planning for roundtable worship in a large assembly dedicated to this understanding of reconciliation requires both an attention to the crucial principles of the roundtable gathering and an ingenious capacity to pursue these values with flexibility. For instance, the judicious use of travelling microphones enables people to participate in large gatherings—like town hall forums, for instance—in ways that were not possible only a few years ago. In a larger gathering a small panel gathered around a round central table might represent the conversation of the whole group. The "talking group" would enact "the Word as conversation" in the midst of a larger group. We can also be attentive to language, symbolism, and many other aspects of roundtable worship that do not depend on size or arrangement of the assembly. What must be resisted, however is a change in arrangements that distorts the circle back into a shoebox or creates a performance stage rather than a circle of participation. Unless we have these principles in place we revert to the one-way and often dominative communication model permeating much of our religious heritage and public life.

In this respect the practice of roundtable worship inverts our usual understanding of the relation of small-group to large-group worship. We usually see the small group as a kind of derivative of the large assembly's worship. Roundtable worship asks us to think of this relationship the other way. The large assembly should be seen properly as a derivative of the smaller circle, much as the church's early life can be seen as the generative microcosm for all our worship—gathered around a table in a symbolic meal, conversing about what we have heard, read, and experienced, praying for communion with God, and anticipating the renewal of all creation.

Language and Symbolism

We are committed to language that engages our actual struggles for just governance in this world of conflict and reconciliation. This is why the language of republics and constitutions replaces that of kings and hereditary power. In addition, we want our language to reflect the equality of all participants at the table, regardless of race, gender identity, sexual orientation, class, and the many other divisions we have erected among us. The divisions of language, social class and education are perhaps the most difficult of all to overcome. Indeed, a worship grounded in conversation as the mirroring of God's trinitarian creativity, may tend to lift up those who have greater verbal or artistic ability and share a common mother tongue. This has always been a feature of religious life. But the power of the circle can also lift us up as listeners, as sharers of earth's riches, as co-participants in a struggle for common ground. The sheer silence of one holding the talking piece can be a powerful invitation to listen and to honor the covenant of the circle. In the face of all these barriers to full participation, we want to embody the invitation "*All are welcome.*" This involves more than gracious and hospitable invitations for people to come to the table. It also requires that our form of worship model the patterns of reconciliation and restoration grounded in the life and spirit of Jesus.

The reconciliation we are trying to live into has many dimensions. It is interpersonal as well as familial. It involves how we make decisions in organizations, whether civil, economic, or political. Reconciliation must constantly be negotiated among competing interest groups and, aggrieved enemies. Courts must address criminal and civil injuries. The language they use in doing this shapes our lives very deeply, whether it is in phrases like "paying his debt to society," "reaching across the aisle," or "being brought to justice." Worship that really seeks to live into God's reconciliation has to select an appropriate language from the competing ways we talk about injury and repair, self-interest and cooperation, rights and obligations. In the movement from patriarchal monarchy to conciliar and covenantal forms of governance we are challenged by new ways of thinking, speaking, and imagining a just life together.

In our own time, as part of a long, long struggle, people around the world are trying to address their conflicts and need for cooperation with some form of republican and democratic order. They are gradually extending these democratic values to women and minorities in their populations. Even today's tyrannies, dictatorships, and repressive theocracies use republican and democratic language in order to claim legitimacy in the eyes of others. Their distortion of the meaning of presidency, democracy, or public order needs to be constantly contested by the ideals lifted up in the language and behavior of roundtable worship. Yet our historic language of prayer and worship still reflects the feudal monarchies that shaped its birth. The church often speaks the language of baronial England rather than today's republics, whether anchored in Washington, Berlin, New Delhi, or Jerusalem. Much of its worship emerges as medieval nostalgia masquerading as genuine Christian eschatological hope. Or it takes up the patterns of performative celebrities from media culture that have corrupted democratic republics and overwhelmed local communities. Not only do these competing models of governing power keep us from addressing our world with a critical alternative; it also keeps us from fully expressing the essential dynamics of circle conversation at the heart of reconciliation at Christ's table.

The struggle for appropriate language and symbolism of God's governance always leads us back to the centrality of prayer language that binds words, emotions, and faith together in profound ways. The challenge to build a better language is not an easy one to address. We struggle with words like "Lord" or "kingdom" that still have a familiar and comforting ring for many of us, even though we would reject their political forms in our everyday life. Unfortunately, in reducing their meaning to interpersonal and familial terms we lose the sense of wider governance and cosmic order grounded in God's purposes. We also struggle with the use of contemporary terms like republics or constitutions that may not have the ring of transcendence or warm familiarity. Even the word "worship" has become a problem for people who feel in it the dead hand of the past rather than the living longing for renewal. Our search for words that transcend gender often leaves us with cumbersome sentences and labored constructions that are ethically sound but verbally unmusical. Though there is a sense of breathing fresh air when the new language of reconciliation clicks, we know we still have a long way to go to unite our worship practices with our ethics and aesthetics.

In spite of these challenges we have decided that it is better to speak than remain silent in the face of mysteries, better to attempt failures in new words rather than entrapment in the old. We know that we are clumsy interlopers in a conversation with a world known more by faith and hope than ear and eye. While we work hard to use songs, prayers, and liturgies that embody our aspirations, we try to be charitable and forbearing, patient and forgiving, as we draw on whatever words we can use to share from the heart with others in conversation and prayer. These virtues, too, are useful for the work of reconciliation!

Gathering as Formation

Every form of worship assumes a prior process of training. We have to be "acculturated" to participate in the "cult."[3] As children, most of us were taught to be quiet and sit still in worship. It cultivated special meanings for standing, sitting, and kneeling, if not dancing and shouting. The more educational patterns of worship formed people in passivity if not receptivity to a presentation. More motivational worship formed us to clapping, shouting, and applause. Some of us learned to sing classical music in harmony. A few of us learned to play keyboard instruments. In a similar way, a roundtable gathering has to assume and provide a process of formation in which we learn to speak briefly but from the heart, listen appreciatively, and be patient in silence. We are formed here to offer not only our money but also our thoughts,

---

3. For a recent exploration of this dynamic, especially in its connection to worship, see Smith, *You Are What You Love*.

prayers, songs, and symbols at the table. This formation is not accomplished solely or even primarily by words, but by movements, symbols, rituals, song, and rhythm. It is an action forming the whole self of body, mind, and spirit.

Formation is not only a process of being steeped in a tradition, but also in personal experiences that are continually reinforced as we gather with others over time. Many of us have already experienced the power of circles, whether in recovery and therapy groups or in mediation and small working groups. We bring those habits and expectations to Roundtable, even as we refine them in light of the wider transcendence we seek to open up in that setting. Sometimes one of us begins to wander in our words, or we do not find the heartfelt center from which to speak. It is at these times that we need the circle steward to care for the work of the circle to give encouragement where needed, restraint where necessary, and respect for silence and listening.

Let us recall the role of the circle steward. The steward is not running the process. This is the work of the Spirit of the circle. The steward is minister to the circle and the Spirit presiding in it. The steward reminds people at the beginning of the conversation about their covenant, about speaking simply from the heart, and about our commitment to attentive listening. The steward is indeed forming the participants for conversation. But the steward is also present to open the way for the Spirit of the table to in-form the assembly around it. At all times, the steward needs to help create a sense of the holy process of the circle, one to which we are constantly needing to be formed and re-formed. This formation in worship occurs not merely for the sake of individual growth but also to help us engage the conflicts around us in a reconciling manner. It is for the sake of our world.

We do not have a formal process to prepare people for this kind of gathering. Most churches give no formal attention to formation for and through worship, so we are not alone in this matter. For us, moreover, there is no initiation process into our commitments or to the circle process, except for our training for circle stewards. Perhaps we need something like this, whether in the form of a study circle or a manual. But we would have to think about whether that would create a barrier rather than an invitation. We need an instructive but also an inviting pathway into the gathering. Perhaps this little book may help in this process.

The limited gathering at table can also play a vital role in forming and reforming the wider church. In a church constituted by voluntary association, church reforms almost always arise out of the leavening work of small groups. Throughout Christian history these groups have continually arisen to breathe new life into the church, often under enormous persecution fostered by the dominant church institutions.

Methodists will see in our gatherings a form of the classes that early Methodists assembled to re-form people in their faith and practice. The Wesley brothers began with a small group of disciplined (methodical!) seekers of a deeper spiritual life which then formed the core of a Christian tradition that has taken many forms over the last 250 years. These class meetings engaged in rigorous self-examination and critical conversation to encourage each other to deepen their interior lives as well as express these spiritual changes in service to others, including social reform.

Moravians might see in our eating and drinking notes of their own "agape meal," or Lovefeast. Like the Moravian practice, this meal is not a formal Eucharist presided over by a representative of the wider church. It is not a meal within the symbolism of sacrifice and divine justice of traditional Church teachings. It does not draw on the sacrificial interpretations of the synoptic Gospel or Pauline accounts. It reflects much more the creation of a new community of mutual self-giving laid out in John's Gospel. It arises in the sharing in food and drink recalled by the simple meal at Emmaus when the disciples recognized the resurrected Christ (Luke 24:30–32) as well as the ongoing table communion of the church throughout its history. It is a rehearsal of the way the Holy Spirit creates a new community, a new conversation, that anticipates a whole new creation. Through the tangible act of eating and drinking we live into the bodily nature of this resurrected life.

THE PLACE OF ROUNDTABLE WORSHIP IN THE WIDER CHURCH

Members of the Society of Friends (the Quakers) will see our circle as a meeting for deep listening to the Spirit. In silence, as in the pause as we pass the talking piece, Friends wait on the illumination of the Spirit in order to speak to one another of their inner leadings. This, too, is a crucial feature of roundtable worship. Likewise, the historic Friends emphasis on persuasion over violence lies at the core of the conversation leading to reconciliation. As Parker Palmer has pointed out, this dynamic of conversation lies at the foundation of democratic life and is vital to the constant renewal of a republic.[4]

Many monastic communities, whether in Catholic, Anglican, or Orthodox traditions, have gathered in circle for Eucharist as well as chapter meetings as a normal part of their worship. I think in particular of the circular chapter room at the great Minster Cathedral in York, England. I also remember the round altar table in the center of a small Norbertine chapel outside Albuquerque, New Mexico. The scope of these kinds of gatherings is wide indeed, though their impact on the wider church has been quite varied.

Finally, I might mention the way that women in the nineteenth century began to claim power in the church by meeting in "circles" of prayer, fellowship, and conversation outside the domination of men in the official church. These circles were seedbeds of many social movements for reform, whether in temperance, abolition, or the care of women forced into bearing children conceived under violent circumstances. In calling their associations "circles" they were claiming the equality of mutuality that escaped them in the hierarchically ordered male-dominated church.

Thus, we gather in an ancient tradition that has persisted in many forms, especially for the renewal of the church. It is a form that can continue to engage the work of reconciliation today. Indeed, we have learned from all of these traditions and more, although at crucial points we also go beyond them. This is especially so in our struggle for language and symbolism that engages forms of justice and reconciliation rooted in a restorative vision. It is a form of reconciliation emerging out of a long process of

---

4. Palmer, *The Company of Strangers*, and many other writings.

argument, investigation, testimony, and prayerful openness to God's mysterious triune life and power.

Diversity at the Table

Like so many churches and associations we lament our lack of cultural, racial, or demographic diversity. In our own time power-seekers in politics and culture use diversity to inflame fear, animosity, and alienation. However, it is diversity that lies at the heart of truly transformative conversation. It is in diversity that the work of reconciliation appears most vividly. Not to have a diverse group at table is to reduce the expansiveness of our vision and our entrée to the world around us. But, as a voluntary association, our diversity tends to be reduced to the boundaries of our local community. Becoming more diverse, as any church or association knows, cannot be a goal in itself but must arise from pursuit of its mission. If the mission—such as witnessing to reconciliation—is taken seriously enough, diversity will arise. Much of this work of diversity emerges in the circle conversations we have spun off from our worship table to address conflicts in our wider community.

However, the more intimate character of the roundtable also militates against attracting the diversity characteristic of more expansive publics. As with any voluntary association, we face the same constraints on taking in the wider pluralism of human life. Sometimes the best we can do is maintain a consciousness and symbolism of this diversity in order to form us for engaging in it. The circle conversation is often more a practice that is brought to the conflicts of a diverse humanity than a table to which diverse people feel welcome.

The Wider Circles of Engagement

We call our worship time a gathering. We gather in response to a call from Christ's table of reconciliation. It is not usually or not yet a time for the transformation of actual conflicts. For that purpose we established for a time a wider umbrella we called Reconciling Conversations. Other roundtable gatherings could find other ways to extend the circle into particular areas of conflict and struggle in the community around them. Through that wider group we have sought to implement the kind of circle conversations and processes Thomas Porter has set forth in *The Spirit and Art of Conflict Transformation*. Drawing on Porter's work with JustPeace, the United Methodist Center for Conflict Transformation, we have conducted training sessions for circle stewards. These in turn can preside at circle conversations in the wider church and community.

Over the past few years we inaugurated circle conversations around difficult issues such as homosexuality and non-binary and transgender identities, war, gun violence, immigration, and racial reparations, as well as church conflict. In bringing people together around issues of immigration or racism, for instance, we automatically engage diversity. This may not appear in the worship gathering that nourishes people engaged in this circle, but the two circles inform each other. The circle dealing with a specific problem in our community is interdependent with the circle gathered at Roundtable. They nurture, inform, and challenge each other.

In particular, roundtable worship seeks to form people for the work of circle conversation and conflict transformation by providing rituals and symbols of and for this work—the hospitable invitation, the circle conversation, the talking piece, the sharing of food, trusting in the Spirit presiding at the table, and grounding our hopes in God's power rather than our own weakness.

Rather than merging these two circles, which might exclude people from both, we pursue a life of interlocking circles with differing special tasks but sharing in the one work of God's reconciliation. Keeping them in a genuine relation of mutual recognition remains an ongoing task, as does the work of cultivating interlocking covenants of mutual understanding and support in the wider church.

The Challenge of Ecological Reconciliation

The reconciliation toward which God calls us is also a reconciliation with God's creation. In the Christian biblical narrative full reconciliation between God and creation is the grace-filled renewal of the original garden. Ecological themes are beginning to appear (or reappear) in Christian worship today, but we are only at the beginning of re-thinking the central theme of reconciliation in terms of our relationship with God's creation.[5] As we think about this in terms of a roundtable worship that takes ecological reconciliation seriously, we have many questions. How do we give other creatures and actors in creation a voice at table? How do we re-imagine our conflicts in terms of struggles over territory, water, energy, and beauty? How do the habits formed by being part of a conversation reshape our understanding as creatures who are members of creation rather than its masters?[6]

At Roundtable we have some small signs of the changes we might need. We place elements of non-human nature at the table in terms of plant, feather, bread, and juice. Sometimes our conversation revolves around ecological themes. The circle itself is rooted in the forms of creation, as Black Elk has reminded us. In assuming that the reconciliation process is rooted in the transformation of conflict, we move away from the simple view that creation is a clock obeying God's laws. Rather, it is an ongoing, living creation whose many expressions of God's creativity are constantly interacting with each other at various levels of power and novelty. Some are as enormous and spectacular as exploding supernovae. Others are as tender and invisible as the love of people who have given life to one another. This is one more example of moving from a theology and world-view shaped by the archaic image of obedience between Father and Son to one rooted in evolving systems shaped by fields of attraction among friends, partners, citizens, and lovers.

5. For some earlier leads see Santmire, *Ritualizing Nature*.

6. For some rich reflections on "the great conversation" with the natural world, drawing on Thomas Berry, Belden Lane, Howard Thurman, and voices from quantum physics as well as her own experience, see Loorz, *Church of the Wild*, chapters 5 and 6.

This systemic view of evolving creation is reflected in the centrality of conversation rather than of one voice preaching the "Word of God." It is also reflected in the priority we give to God's abundance in creation over our own often failing efforts to progress to moral perfection. It is a perspective rooted not in pyramids of domination but in circles of interaction. In this respect, the image of the triune God underlying our conversational circle reflects a view of the world that stresses membership and participation rather than exploitation and mastery. Such a change in mindset is crucial to living into a sustainable future. These are only small steps in our symbolic and intellectual worlds. The challenge of living into an ecological understanding of reconciliation confronts us all. We believe that in the roundtable gathering we have a peculiar possibility for addressing this challenge in the years ahead.

Interfaith Worship in the Abrahamic Traditions

While our own form of roundtable worship is clearly rooted in Christian tradition, it also has ancestors and relatives in the other Abrahamic traditions. The Jewish High Holy Days provide one example. The passage from the new beginnings proclaimed at Rosh Hashana to the reflections and repentance of the subsequent days of Tsuvah ("turning," similar to the Greek Christian term of *metanoia*) and then to the celebration of forgiveness and reconciliation in Yom Kippur shares a paradigm common to the two traditions. Certainly, the tradition of table and conversation are deeply rooted among Jews of all persuasions! We also need to explore points in Muslim worship, such as the fasts and feasts of Ramadan, where roundtable forms might gain fresh expression. The Sufi tradition seems to be especially rich in ways to express the underlying conversation of God and creation.

At its core, roundtable worship offers basic elements for interfaith dialogue that still need to be explored. This is a pathway that can be rich in new relationships, understandings, and commitments to building up bonds of reconciliation in our violent age. A number of people have been exploring how the image of

Abraham's tent of hospitality in Genesis 18 provides an invitation for people in the Abrahamic tradition to come together at table in conversation and nurture.[7] We have only begun to touch the door handles to this wider work.

The Way Forward

Our Roundtable gatherings have constituted a journey as well as a process of constructing a new home for worship in the broad Christian tradition. Some elements have become fairly stable. Other features stand as boundary questions—of size, diversity, language, formation, the ecological character of God's work of reconciliation, and the opening to interfaith collaboration. They contain possibilities and pathways we are only beginning to address. They require entry into a wider conversation, which I hope this little book will stimulate.

This form of worship recommends itself as the nucleus of Christian worship as well as a fundamental public within God's greater republics of church and world. It sings the song of God's reconciliation at the core of our worship, but it does so in a new key. By focusing on the Holy Spirit's work at the roundtable, it moves us away from an excessive preoccupation with the sacrificial contest of fathers and sons and from the monarchs and patriarchs of earlier forms of governance. By focusing on God's nurturing goodness at table it builds up our capacity to help each other in our weakness and limited vision. By forming us for conversation in circles of mutual respect it helps us forge new covenants and relationships deeper than legal conformity.

Roundtable can be a worship gathering in any church in addition to traditional or contemporary forms. It would lift up for people a way of coming to Christ's table that is also engaged with the practices of reconciliation, conflict transformation, and peacebuilding emerging all over the globe. From it can flow practices that

---

7. See Waskow, Chittister, and Chisti, *The Tent of Abraham*.

can influence both the other worship gatherings as well as ways of transforming conflicts in the church and its communities.

The various Christian traditions may well find that roundtable worship both resonates with and also clashes with particular features in their own heritage. It is obvious that we cannot solve these age-old differences and divisions here. I have only tried to set forth our own practices and a theological framework for engaging in them, hoping that others can find ways that they can be related in a vital manner to their own traditions without sacrificing the crucial elements of the roundtable experience. The roundtable gathering is a powerful pattern of worship rooted in ancient traditions and contemporary commitments. It carries the possibility of re-forming us for the work of reconciliation in our sorely troubled world, longing for its fulfilment in God's new creation.

Appendix: A Roundtable Liturgy

Lighting the Candle
    We light this candle in the name of the God who creates life,
        in the name of the Savior who loves life,
        in the name of the Spirit who is the fire of life.

Call to the Table
    In the darkest night
        We see a light of hope.
    In the chaos of an oceanic fury
        We behold creation of a world of peace.
    In the silence of an empty universe
        We hear a word of welcome.
    In the wailing of a new-born babe,
        We hear the song of everlasting life.
    In a shelter for abandoned lives
        We find a table of thanksgiving.
    ALL: We come to your table of thanks and peace.

A Song of Invocation
    "Star Child," *The Faith We Sing*, 2095

Remembrance (Unison)

> From the garden banished we set out upon the road of toil and grief.
>
> In cave and wilderness a daily bread brought disciplines of humble faithfulness.
>
> Beset by overlords and despots we were led by flickering stars of hope.
>
> In a stable we received an unexpected life of everlasting joy.
>
> In the dark before the dawn we heard the shepherd's faithful call,
>
> In the rising sun, the garden bursting with a newfound beauty.
>
> Amen. Amin. Ameyn

Thanksgiving (Unison)

> O God of Everlasting Life,
>
> For the love that brought us into life, we give you thanks. For babes renewing life in spite of all our fears we give you hearty thanks. For the bounty of your earth and the nurture at your table, we speak forth our gratitude. For each breath we open up our lips in songs of thanks and praise:
>
> Thank You, God, Holy One.
>
> Thank You God Creator,* Thank You God.
>
> > *Redeemer, Great Spirit

Nurture by Bread and Drink

> "The bread of Life"
>
> "The cup of Reconciliation"

Readings

> The Magnificat of Hannah, I Samuel 2:1–10
>
> The Magnificat of Mary, Luke 1:46–55

The Conversation: "What are Hannah and Mary saying to us today?"

Sounding the Bowl

APPENDIX: A ROUNDTABLE LITURGY

Gathered Prayers

The Hope Prayer

    O Source of Life, You alone are holy.

    Come, govern us in perfect peace.

    Give us today the food that we need.

    Release us from our sin as we release our enemies.

    Sustain us in our times of trial.

    Liberate us all from evil powers.

    Guide us in your justice, wisdom, and peace.

    Amen, Amin, Ameyn

Reflective Moment

Words of Commitment

    In God's love, we will seek the path of reconciliation.

    In God's power, we will walk the ways of peace.

    In God's wisdom, we will struggle for God's justice in this world.

    In God's mercy, we will seek to care for Earth, our home.

Blessing Song

    Go now in peace, blessing and blessed,

        Grounded in God, healing and whole.

    Go now in peace, blessing and blessed,

        Grounded in God, filled with God's love.

Bibliography

Allen, Ronald J. "The Power to Resist Empire: You Are What You Worship. Identity, Power, and Mission in the Book of Revelation." In Johnson and Wymer, eds., *Worship and Power*, 25-40.
Arendt, Hannah. *The Human Condition*. Garden City: Doubleday, 1959.
———. *On Revolution*. New York: Viking, 1965.
Ayre, Clive W., and Ernst M. Conradie, eds. *The Church in God's Household: Protestant Perspectives on Ecclesiology and Ecology*. Pietermaritzburg: Cluster, 2016.
Barkat, Amiram. "Prison dig reveals church that may be the oldest in the world." *Ha'aretz* (Tel Aviv), November 6, 2005.
Cobb, John B. Jr. *Process Theology as Political Theology*. Philadelphia: Westminster, 1982.
Deutsch, Karl W. *The Nerves of Government: Models of Communication and Control*. New York: Free Press, 1966.
Duck Ruth, ed. *Flames of the Spirit: Resources for Worship*. New York: Pilgrim, 1985.
Elazar, Daniel J. *The Covenant Tradition in Politics*. 4 volumes. New Brunswick, NJ: Transaction, 1994-1998.
Everett, William Johnson. *God's Federal Republic: Reconstructing our Governing Symbol*. Mahweh, NJ: Paulist, 1988; reprint Eugene, OR: Wipf and Stock, 2019.
———. *Making My Way in Ethics, Worship, and Wood: An Expository Memoir*. Eugene, OR: Resource Publications, 2021.
———. *The Politics of Worship: Reforming the Language and Symbols of Liturgy*. Cleveland: United Church, 1999.
———. *Religion, Federalism, and the Struggle for Public Life: Cases from Germany, India, and America*. New York: Oxford University Press, 1997.
Granfield, Patrick. *Ecclesial Cybernetics*. New York: Macmillan, 1973.
Habermas, Jürgen. *The Theory of Communicative Action*. 2 vols. Translated by Thomas McCarthy. Boston: Beacon, 1985 and 1992.

BIBLIOGRAPHY

Hartshorne, Charles. *The Divine Relativity: A Social Conception of God.* New Haven: Yale University Press, 1948, 1982.

James, William. *A Pluralistic Universe.* Cambridge, MA: Harvard University Press, 1977.

Johnson, Elizabeth. *She Who Is: The Mystery of God in Feminist Theological Discourse.* New York: Crossroad, 1992.

Johnson, Sarah Kathleen, and Andrew Wymer. "Introduction: Liturgical Authority in Free Church Traditions." In Johnson and Wymer, eds., *Worship and Power*, 1-22.

Johnson, Sarah Kathleen, and Andrew Wymer, eds. *Worship and Power: Liturgical Authority in Free Church Traditions.* Eugene, OR: Cascade, 2023.

Lederach, John Paul. *The Little Book of Conflict Transformation.* Intercourse, PA: Good Books, 2003.

LaCugna, Catherine Mowry. *God for Us: The Trinity and Christian Life.* San Francisco: Harper, 1973.

Loorz, Victoria. *Church of the Wild: How Nature Invites Us into the Sacred.* Minneapolis: Broadleaf Books, 2021.

Marshall, Christopher D. *Beyond Retribution: A New Testament Vision for Justice, Crime, and Punishment.* Grand Rapids, MI: Eerdmans, 2001.

McCaslin, Wanda D., ed. *Justice as Healing: Indigenous Ways.* St. Paul, MN: Living Justice, 2005.

McFague, Sallie. *Models of God: Theology for an Ecological, Nuclear Age.* Philadelphia: Fortress, 1987.

"Megiddo Church Israel." https://en.wikipedia.org/wiki/Megiddo_church_Israel.

Moltmann, Jürgen. *The Spirit of Life: A Universal Affirmation.* Minneapolis: Fortress, 2001.

Müller-Fahrenholz, Geiko. *God's Spirit: Transforming a World in Crisis.* New York: Continuum, 1995.

Murray, John Courtney. *We Hold These Truths: Catholic Reflections on the American Proposition.* New York: Sheed and Ward, 1960.

Myers, Henry. *Medieval Kingship.* Chicago: Nelson-Hall, 1982.

Neihardt, John G. *Black Elk Speaks: The Complete Edition.* Lincoln, NE: University of Nebraska Press, 2014.

Newsom, Carol, Sharon Ringe, and Jacqueline Lapsley, eds. *Women's Bible.* Third edition, revised and updated. Louisville, KY: Westminster/John Knox, 2012.

Palmer, Parker. *The Company of Strangers: Christians and the Renewal of America's Public Life.* New York: Herder and Herder, 1983.

Porter, Thomas. *The Spirit and Art of Conflict Transformation: Creating a Culture of JustPeace.* Nashville, TN: Upper Room, 2010.

Porter, Thomas, ed. *Conflict and Communion: Reconciliation and Restorative Justice at Christ's Table.* Nashville, TN: Discipleship Resources, 2006.

Pranis, Kay. *The Little Book of Circle Processes: A New/Old Approach to Peacemaking.* Intercourse, PA: Good Books, 2005.

Rohr, Richard. *Dancing Standing Still: Healing the World from a Place of Prayer.* Mahwah, NJ: Paulist, 2014.

Rohr, Richard, with Mike Morrell. *The Divine Dance: The Trinity and Your Transformation.* New Kensington, PA: Whitaker, 2020.

Ruether, Rosemary Radford. *Gaia and God: An Ecofeminist Theology of Earth Healing.* San Francisco: Harper-Collins, 1992.

Russell, Letty. *Church in the Round: Feminist Interpretation of the Church.* Louisville, KY: Westminster/John Knox, 1993.

Santmire, H. Paul. *Ritualizing Nature: Renewing Christian Liturgy in a Time of Crisis.* Minneapolis: Fortress, 2008.

Schneiders, Sandra. *Women and the Word: The Gender of God in the New Testament and the Spirituality of Women.* Mahwah, NJ: Paulist, 1986.

Schüssler-Fiorenza, Elisabeth. *In Memory of Her: A Feminist Theological Reconstruction of Christian Origins.* New York: Herder and Herder, 1994.

———. *Wisdom Ways: Introducing Feminist Biblical Interpretation.* Maryknoll, NY: Orbis, 2001.

Smith, C. Christopher. *How the Body of Christ Talks: Recovering the Practice of Conversation in the Church.* Grand Rapids, MI: Brazos, 2019.

Smith, James K. A. *You Are What You Love: The Spiritual Power of Habit.* Grand Rapids, MI: Brazos, 2016.

———. *Desiring the Kingdom: Worship, Worldview, and Cultural Formation.* "Cultural Liturgies," vol. 1. Grand Rapids, MI: Baker, 2009.

———. *Imagining the Kingdom: How Worship Works.* "Cultural Liturgies," vol. 2. Grand Rapids, MI: Baker, 2013.

———. *Awaiting the King: Reforming Public Theology.* "Cultural Liturgies," vol. 3. Grand Rapids, MI: Baker, 2017.

Stackhouse, Max L. *Ethics and the Urban Ethos: An Essay in Social Theory and Theological Reconstruction.* Boston: Beacon, 1972.

Suchocki, Marjorie Hewitt. *God, Christ, Church: A Practical Guide to Process Theology.* New York: Crossroad, 1982, 1989.

Swimme, Brian, and Thomas Berry. *The Universe Story: From the Primordial Flaring Forth to the Ecozoic Era—A Celebration of the Unfolding of the Cosmos.* San Francisco: Harper, 1992.

Teilhard de Chardin, Pierre, "Mass on the World," in *Hymn of the Universe,* translated by Gerald Vann, OP. New York: Harper and Row, 1965, 19–37.

———. *The Phenomenon of Man.* Translated by Bernard Wall. New York: Harper and Row, 1965.

Waskow, Arthur and Joan Chittister, MSS, and Murshid Saadi Shakur Chishti. *The Tent of Abraham: Stories of Hope and Peace for Jews, Christians, and Muslims.* Boston: Beacon, 2007.

Welker, Michael. *God the Spirit.* Translated by John Hoffmeyer. Minneapolis: Fortress, 1994.

Wren, Brian. *What Language Shall I Borrow? God-talk in Worship: A Male Response to Feminist Theology.* New York: Crossroad, 1989.

Zehr, Howard. *The Little Book of Restorative Justice.* Intercourse, PA: Good Books, 2002.

www.ingramcontent.com/pod-product-compliance
Lightning Source LLC
Chambersburg PA
CBHW070455090426
42735CB00012B/2563